MORE
WITH
LESS

MORE WITH LESS

Whole Food Cooking
Made Irresistibly Simple

JODI MORENO

ROOST
BOULDER
2018

CONTENTS

Introduction

My mother was incredibly hardworking, more so than anyone else I have ever known. Despite the long hours she would work as a nurse, she somehow managed to serve us a home-cooked meal every single night. Dinnertime was *the meal* at our house and was something I always looked forward to. It wasn't until I went away to college that I realized how much I took my mother's cooking for granted and that it was not necessarily easy, fast, or convenient to cook for yourself or your family every day. Fast food and cafeteria food ruled my life through those years, and I often yearned for simple comforts of home like my mom's nourishing lentil soup or her delicious eggplant rollatini.

It took a few years of living away from home to learn that, if I wanted to eat home-cooked food often, I needed to learn how to cook for myself. I would call up my mom to ask for recipes like stuffed artichokes and attempt to make them in my tiny, ill-equipped kitchen. Even though my food was not very good and certainly never tasted like my mom's, I discovered that the kitchen was my happy place.

Years went by, my love for cooking grew, and my culinary repertoire expanded beyond my mother's tried-and-true favorites. I became obsessed with reading recipes and particularly intrigued by unique flavor combinations. When I got home from work, I would spend hours re-creating elaborate recipes from a cookbook that I picked out the weekend before. The next day, I would bring the leftovers in to my coworkers, who would always jokingly say that I should be working in a kitchen, not an office. One year I brought a crispy Brussels sprout dish for a holiday office party—it had sautéed apples and shallots and some toasted walnuts, and was tossed in Dijon mustard, olive oil, and a splash of red wine vinegar. So many of my coworkers asked for the recipe that it set off a spark inside me to create more of my own original recipes. Very soon after, I started my blog, enrolled in culinary school, and here we are.

I get great joy from thinking outside the box when I cook, and I strongly believe there is a powerful connection between food and our overall health and well-being. When you take the time to cook for yourself and your family, you realize the importance of selecting the very best ingredients to use in your kitchen. By cooking with whole, local, organic produce whenever possible, you are doing your very best to nourish yourself and those you are feeding.

After a hectic day in our busy lives, it can be tempting to pick up takeout or to pop a packaged frozen meal in the oven. My hope is that this book inspires you to cook more often and gives you the tools to make simple, wholesome, delicious meals almost any day of the week.

KEEPING IT SIMPLE

My culinary training is in natural foods with an emphasis on plant-based cooking and nutrition. Of the many things I learned in school, focusing on how the ingredients and the cooking techniques we choose can enrich our life and directly affect our health and well-being has had the greatest impact on me and the recipes I create.

Prior to my training, even though I considered myself a "healthy" eater, I was someone who thought that a meal was not complete unless it had some form of cheese or animal protein. I became fascinated by what I saw as a challenge—using less cheese, bread, and meat when creating recipes for flavorful meals. What I quickly learned was that using fewer of those ingredients opened up a world of tasty, exciting, and more nourishing foods that I never knew existed. I loved learning more ways to incorporate vegetables, grains, legumes, nuts, and seeds in every single meal. I also became much more in tune with eating with the seasons, and discovered that is it less about avoiding certain ingredients and more about taking advantage of the amazing colorful array of whole foods I encountered year-round at the farmers' market. Even in the deep winter, when all I can find at the markets are root vegetables for months and months, my creativity thrives on making the most out of what is available.

Through embracing seasonal produce, healthier ingredients, and overall simplicity, I have discovered that there is a beauty in highlighting one main ingredient or just a couple of ingredients that pair together in perfect harmony. When you try to make more out of less, something magical happens. Quality ingredients get to do what they do best—shine and complement one another as they were meant to. You really can get the most out of everyday cooking when recipes are simplified and pared down to only the most essential ingredients and preparations.

While there is certainly a time and place for more advanced techniques, or recipes with a long list of ingredients, there can be an elegance found in simplicity. As much as I love to spend hours wandering aisles in the grocery store or experimenting in my kitchen, busy everyday life does not always afford us that luxury. I truly believe that when cooking is as delicious as it is approachable, we are all more likely to incorporate it into our regular routines.

HOW I LIKE TO EAT

First and foremost, I adore quality ingredients that are sourced as close to my home as possible. If it is not growing in my backyard, I head to the farmers' market to get as much as I can there, and later fill in any odds and ends at the grocery store. I am fortunate enough to live near year-round farmers' markets, which is something I do not take for granted.

I am not a big fan of diets or food labels. Throughout the years, after so much research and trying (and not trying) different things, I have found that my body is happiest when I stay away from processed food, gluten, soy, and dairy (cow's milk); when I minimize my sugar intake; and especially when I am eating lots and lots of vegetables and whole grains. Since my approach to eating is more about feeling my best, and I do not have any debilitating food allergies, I tend to leave wiggle room for when I want a delicious piece of apple pie with ice cream (with all the gluten and all the dairy). I know that if I eat the way my body prefers 80 to 90 percent of the time, I do not need to stress about indulging once in a while. I do eat meat but not nearly as often as I eat vegetables. When I do cook it at home I like to know where it came from, what it was eating, and how it was treated. Same goes with fish. We eat a decent amount of fish because we live on the coast and fresh fish is plentiful, so it's that much easier to choose fish that is wild-caught, local, and sustainable.

The recipes in this book are a reflection of how I like to eat day to day. While everything you find here has the option of being dairy-, gluten-, and soy-free, you will also find that I like to keep things flexible and make a few exceptions. Miso, a friendlier version of soy thanks to the fermentation process, is one of my favorite ingredients and one you will find often throughout the book. However, there's always an option to use a chickpea- or brown rice–based miso if you want to keep it soy-free. Same for ghee—my favorite ingredient for sautéing. Ghee is considered dairy because it is a clarified butter, but I find it much easier to digest than regular butter, and it is perfect for sautéing with its high smoke point. If you are dairy-free, there is always an option to use olive oil, coconut oil, or a neutral oil such as sunflower instead.

Ultimately, cooking should be fun, approachable, and celebrated, and not just on special occasions but as a part of a daily routine. After all, the food you eat should make you happy, and if it makes you feel great too, well, that's the (dairy-free) icing on the cake.

HOW TO USE THIS BOOK

Instinct is such a key component of cooking, and the very same recipe can taste quite different depending on who made it. With that in mind, I've designed many of the recipes in this book to be versatile and forgiving. If you are missing a specific ingredient, I often make suggestions for something that could easily take its place. Except for the baking recipes, almost all the recipes can be altered to your tastes or what you have on hand. You might like a little more of a certain herb or spice, so feel free to have a heavy (or light) hand when you are in the mood. If you know you love lemon, go ahead and give a dish that extra squeeze. If you prefer to take it easy on the garlic, use less than I suggest.

While there are a few recipes in this book that stick strictly to their season (such as stews in the winter), many can be altered to be used year-round depending on what you find at your local market. Again, it is all about experimenting and having fun. If you see that a recipe calls for squash and you can only find sweet potato, don't be afraid to give it a try.

I tend to think of my recipes as simple equations, and I love to add one, two, or three ingredients together, especially when I think that they would enhance one another. Sometimes this is for a contrast of texture (a smooth soup with a crunchy topping) or flavor (salty and sweet, or a pop of acidity). Finding complementary ingredients whether for flavor or texture is a trick that can elevate any meal, and using a simple equation makes it easier to find substitutes when needed, or just for fun. When you want to incorporate a crunchy element, try out different ingredients—perhaps some sesame seeds, toasted nuts, or crispy baked quinoa bread crumbs. Or if you're looking for a pop of acidity such as lemon juice, you might try apple cider vinegar or white wine vinegar instead. Some of the best meals are the ones that are improvisational, and my hope is that with these simple, straightforward recipes, making substitutions will be that much easier and intuitive.

The Pantry

———

The pantry is where meal planning really begins. Having a well-stocked, whole foods pantry will make it so much easier for you to cook nourishing meals on a daily basis, and will minimize runs to the grocery store for last-minute ingredients. At the same time, an overly crowded pantry will mean more things get lost in the back of the cupboard, past their expiration date. It is fairly easy to achieve a healthy balance so that your pantry becomes an inspiration or touchstone for your daily meals.

I often come up with ideas for recipes just from looking through my pantry and spotting an ingredient I haven't used in a while, or finding a little something in the spice rack that will give a soup that extra zing. And your pantry is not just about the foods that sit in the cupboard—it is also the fridge, the freezer, the countertop, and maybe even your backyard. I think of the pantry as whatever ingredients you have that are easily accessible and kept within arm's length for whipping up a nourishing, flavorful meal.

My kitchen staples include many of the more common items such as olive oil, cumin, and peanut butter, but it also includes some less-common ingredients that I have found to be crucial in a well-stocked kitchen. Ingredients such as ghee (clarified butter) for sautéing and kombu (a type of seaweed) for making stocks have transformed my cooking and made it even easier for me to produce complex, layered flavors with minimal effort. Here are my suggestions for a well-balanced, interesting (but not overstuffed) pantry.

COOKING FATS + FINISHING OILS

One of the most used sections of my pantry contains the cooking fats and finishing oils. It is important to have a wide variety of cooking oils, because not all oils and fats are created equal or do the same job.

> **Extra Virgin Olive Oil** I love to use this as a finishing oil or for lower-heat sautéing and roasting. I prefer olive oils with a tangy, strong flavor and a fruit finish.
> **Coconut Oil** This is a favorite for baked goods and occasionally for sautéing—just be aware that it leaves behind a subtle coconut flavor.
> **Ghee** This clarified butter is great for sautéing over high heat because of its high smoke point (the temperature at which the oil begins to burn, giving

food a burned flavor and losing nutritional benefits). It also adds a lovely richness and subtle nutty, buttery flavor.

Sunflower, Grapeseed, and Canola Oils These neutral oils are ideal for sautéing over high heat or for frying because of their high smoke point.

Grass-fed Butter I use butter sparingly, for an occasional low-heat sauté when I want that added richness to a dish or for the miso butter recipes (page 27).

Toasted Sesame Oil I use this purely as a finishing oil, for drizzling over vegetables and noodles or mixed in salad dressings and sauces. It is best paired with typically Asian ingredients such as rice vinegar and tamari (or soy sauce or coconut aminos).

VINEGARS / CITRUS

Vinegars and the acidity from citrus can add a wonderful depth of flavor and really bring out the other flavors in a dish. While vinegars and acid are commonly used in salad dressings and condiments, many recipes, especially soups, can benefit from a squeeze of lemon or a splash of red wine vinegar. While I tend to use lemon juice and apple cider vinegar the most since they are so nutritionally beneficial, sherry vinegar, red wine vinegar, and white wine vinegar are standouts in some of my recipes.

Apple Cider Vinegar With its ability to lower blood sugar, this is one of the most healthful of the vinegars, and it has so many wonderful uses. Outside of using it to balance out a dressing or add a punch of acidity to a soup, I sometimes like to add a teaspoon to a cup of tea for its alkalizing effect on the body.

Brown Rice Vinegar This vinegar works best in Asian dressings and sauces, such as a ginger-based salad dressing or a peanut sauce.

White Wine Vinegar This is my go-to vinegar for salad dressings or for punching up roasted vegetables, soups, and sauces.

Sherry Vinegar I keep a good-quality sherry vinegar around because of its tangy, fruity, sophisticated flavor profile. It is a key component in one of my favorite salad dressings (on page 39), but I also love to splash it over warm sautéed veggies.

Red Wine Vinegar Another excellent vinegar for dressings and sometimes soups, it is also the key ingredient in the Chimichurri + Yogurt recipe (page 32).

Champagne Vinegar This is a bright, fruit-forward vinegar to splash over salad greens with some olive oil.

Lemon A squeeze of lemon juice can add brightness and depth of flavor to just about anything—soups, salads, roasted or grilled vegetables, even a cup of tea. I always have lemons on hand.

Lime I love the bright hit of fruity acid from any citrus, but limes have their own unique flavor and are perfect for peanut sauce and guacamole.

SALTS

Salt is essential for bringing out the best in a dish. At the same time, there is a delicate balance between being perfectly seasoned and oversalted. Everyone's tastes are different, which is why it is especially important to taste along the way. I go light on the salt in the beginning—you can always add more, but you cannot take it away. Try using a variety of salts for their flavor and texture differences as well as for the various minerals. No matter which type is called for, feel free to use the salt of your choice—just keep in mind that kosher salt tastes saltier than all the other salts, so adjust accordingly.

Sea Salt This is the salt called for most often in this book. It has a finer grain and is less "salty" than kosher salt, making it an easy, versatile salt.

Kosher Salt I like to think of it as the bad boy of salts: it has a thicker grain and the strongest "salt" taste. I use it more sparingly because there is not much nutritional value, but when you really need that punchy salt taste to come through, it is a great choice.

Himalayan Sea Salt I use this salt the most because it has more than eighty trace minerals, including potassium and magnesium. Although I do not specify it in the ingredients for my recipes, it can be used wherever sea salt is used, in the same amount.

Maldon Sea Salt This is used purely for finishing. It has a wonderful texture, and adds a salty crunch to anything you sprinkle it on.

SWEETENERS

While I like to keep overall sugar use to a minimum, there are times (hello, dessert!) when a little sugar is welcomed with open arms. When I do use a sweetener, I stick to the more natural, lower glycemic sugars, such a maple syrup, honey, and coconut palm sugar, but you will see the occasional use of good ole white sugar in my recipes.

Coconut Palm Sugar I use this sugar in most of my baked goods because it is less processed and has a lower glycemic index that regular white granulated sugar; however, it does give a brown tint to whatever it is

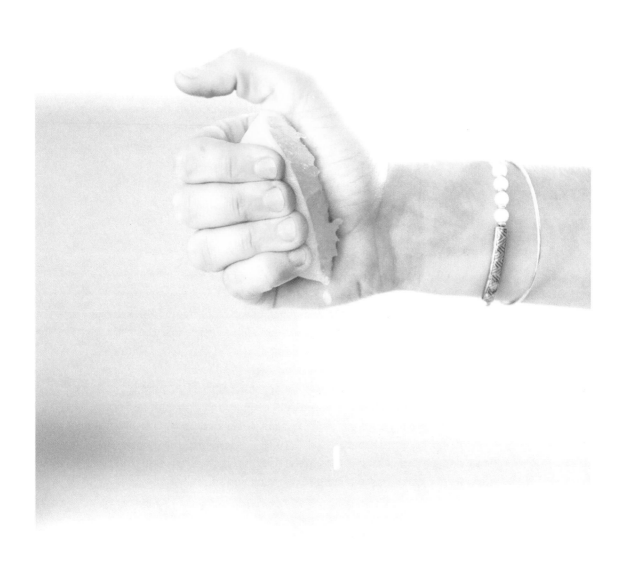

added to, so keep that in mind if you're ever subbing it for white sugar.

Maple Syrup This is my favorite sweetener—it has a low glycemic index, and I love its cozy maple flavor. It works well in baked goods, as well as in ice cream and other frozen desserts.

Honey I use this for a sweet boost in things such as yogurt, oatmeal, and teas.

White Granulated Sugar It can be hard to replace the taste, texture, and color of regular white granulated sugar, which is why you will see it in a couple of recipes in this book. I like it for cakes that wouldn't look as good with a brown tint (from coconut sugar or maple syrup). You can interchange coconut sugar and white sugar with a 1:1 ratio in any recipe that calls for either.

Brown Rice Syrup I use this sweetener less often than others, but I like to keep it around because it is super-sticky (stickier than honey!), which is best for holding things together, such as the Apricot + Toasted Coconut Breakfast Bars (page 49).

UMAMI

The wonderful world of umami opens up our tastes buds and gives us that amazing complexity of flavor. That "why does this taste so good?" flavor is usually thanks to an umami ingredient. These are some of the things I keep stocked to give foods that umami boost.

Tamari / Coconut Aminos Since I tend to avoid soy, which is a key umami flavor, I use coconut aminos to get the same effect. Tamari, which is basically soy sauce made without wheat (making it gluten-free), is a close alternative and is much easier to find than coconut aminos.

Tomato Paste It might be the lesser known in the umami category, but it adds a lovely depth of flavor and complexity to certain foods, such as soup broths and tomato-based dishes.

Miso (White, Red, Chickpea) The one exception I make for soy is miso, because the fermentation process results in a much friendlier form of soy, meaning it is less allergenic and has more beneficial amino acids. I like to keep multiple flavors of miso on hand because I use it so often. Sweet miso and red barley miso are my two staples, and would be a good place to start before adding in others as you get more excited about using miso. Of course, if you are avoiding soy altogether, you will want to seek out a soy-free miso such as chickpea.

Shiitake Mushrooms (Dried or Fresh) I always keep dried mushrooms in my pantry because they last forever, are an easy way to add flavor to a dish, and can be used to make a super-nutritious tea when you feel a cold coming on (see page 152). Fresh shiitake mushrooms are also a great ingredient because they easily add umami flavor to a sauté and can hold in moisture (in, for instance, both the Quinoa + Mushroom + Beet Burgers on page 179 and the Coconut Curry Lentilballs on page 192).

Seaweeds (Kombu + Nori) These are not only umami boosters; they also contain a lot of trace minerals that are not found in other foods. I like to use nori for added flavor in condiments, and I use kombu to enhance broths without having to add extra salt.

Anchovies I know these are not necessarily everyone's favorite, but after some convincing, they have become one of mine. Mince them and add to sauces for that salty, umami element like no other.

SPICES

The spice rack is one place where I find a lot of inspiration. It's also a place where I feel like there is always room to add more. While I usually stick to more commonly used spices in my recipes, it is fun to seek more rare spices as well, such as sumac, for experimenting and allowing my tastes to try something new and exciting. With that said, the spices listed here are my preferred and most frequently used, and the ones you will find throughout this book.

- Cumin (ground + seeds)
- Coriander (ground + seeds)
- Turmeric (ground + fresh)
- Curry Powder
- Chili Powder
- Paprika

- Smoked Paprika
- Garlic Powder
- Cayenne
- Red Pepper Flakes
- Mustard (ground + seeds)
- Black Pepper (ground + whole peppercorns)

- Dried Sage, Rosemary, Thyme
- Cinnamon (ground + sticks)
- Nutmeg
- Cloves (ground + whole)
- Star Anise
- Cardamom

DAIRY + DAIRY SUBSTITUTES

While I try to stay away from dairy as much as possible, I do allow a little room for an occasional goat's or sheep's milk cheese or yogurt, as well as grass-fed butter. Coconut products are a lifesaver for those who avoid dairy. Also, nut milks and nut cheeses are some of my favorite dairy-free substitutions. I usually make my own nut milks and cheeses (you will find recipes throughout the book), but these days it is easy to find nut milks and sometimes even nut cheeses in the grocery store.

Canned Coconut Milk I often use coconut milk instead of dairy as a base for sauces, curries, and ice cream, as well as in smoothies and as a whipped dessert topping.

Coconut Manna (Butter) This has a thick, spreadable consistency, making it nice to spread over toast. It is also great to add to smoothies.

Coconut Yogurt I use this as a replacement for cow's milk yogurt. Because most store-bought coconut yogurts have a noticeable coconut flavor, they are best used in dishes that are sweet.

Nut Milk (or any of the milks on pages 70 to 71) I use any kind of nut and seed milk instead of cow's milk in cereal and oatmeal, in coffee and tea, in soups and sauces, as well as for just drinking on its own.

Sheep's or Goat's Milk, Cheese, and Yogurt I don't use these often, but they work really well in a yogurt-based sauce or when I want to make labneh (page 232).

FLOURS + OTHER BAKING SUPPLIES

Flours are used mostly in baked goods, but they are also handy for thickening up a sauce or making a batter for frying. Since I avoid gluten, I use a variety of flours to replace white flour, but I also like to keep it simple so I do not have ten different flours crowding my pantry. After many years of experimenting with alternative flours, the five that follow are the ones I use often and consistently.

Chickpea Flour I use this in savory baked goods, batters, and in the Chickpea Crepes (page 67).

Oat Flour This is the flour I use most often in my baked goods, typically along with a mixture of almond flour and brown rice flour.

Almond Flour This is another flour I use frequently in baked goods. You can make your own almond (or oat) flour easily (which is more affordable than buying prepackaged) by grinding skinless almonds in a food processor or blender until a fine meal is formed.

Brown Rice Flour I use this often in combination with the oat and almond flours when baking.

Gluten-free Flour Blend This blend is good to keep on hand for easily subbing out white flour (1:1) in recipes that you want to make gluten-free, although you will find it in only a couple of recipes in this book.

Cacao Powder This is less processed and therefore more nutritious than cocoa powder; however, it has a more bitter taste. Add it to smoothies or stir it into porridge—just be sure to balance it with a little sweetness.

Cocoa Powder Less nutritious but with a sweeter, chocolatier flavor than cacao, cocoa powder is great to use in baked goods for a rich, chocolaty result.

Psyllium Husks These are a new staple in my pantry, not only because they are great for your digestive system but because they work really well to thicken yogurt or to bind gluten-free bread.

Chocolate Bars (70% to 80% dark) These are well-stocked in my pantry for baked goods, for melting and drizzling, as well as just for snacking.

Coconut Flakes These make a great topping in both sweet and savory dishes, but I also love having coconut flakes on hand for making things such as granola or macaroons.

Chia Seeds These absorbent little seeds are super-nutritious and are high in omegas and other nutrients, which makes them great to add to smoothies or to sprinkle over veggies or salads. They also make a fantastic vegan egg replacer.

Flax Seeds These are also very nutritious and high in fiber, making them ideal for sprinkling and adding to dressings. When ground, they also make a good egg replacer.

Baking Powder This leavening agent helps add volume to baked goods.

Baking Soda Also a leavening agent, baking soda is used only when an acid is present in the recipe (such as lemon juice or apple cider vinegar). The acid is needed to cause the reaction that makes things rise and also to neutralize its flavor.

GRAINS + RICE + LEGUMES

Gluten-free grains and rice are key staples in my pantry. They also last a few months, making it that much easier to throw together a substantial dinner on the fly.

Quinoa With many of the qualities of a grain, quinoa is actually a seed, and therefore a good gluten-free option. It is nutritious and packed with protein, which will give you long-lasting energy. It is also versatile and adapts well to any flavor you add to it. Serve it as a porridge for breakfast, mixed into soups or salads for lunch, and as a side dish for dinner.

Buckwheat I typically use buckwheat as a breakfast porridge when I want to break up my oatmeal routine.

Polenta or Cornmeal When cooked until creamy, it is an extremely warming and filling accompaniment, especially to roasted vegetables.

Millet This is another versatile grain that I like to use interchangeably with quinoa. It too is packed with protein.

Oats I use oats often, and beyond oatmeal. They are handy for binding things such as the Quinoa + Mushroom + Beet Burgers (page 179) and the Coconut Curry Lentilballs (page 192). You can also easily turn rolled oats into oat flour by blitzing them in the food processor or blender and using them in baked goods.

Rice: Brown, White (Short and Long Grain), and Black Rice is our standard accompaniment for dinnertime meals, but I also love to use it in more creative ways, such as in salads or desserts.

Green Split Peas These are easily whipped up into a nutritious soup.

Lentils (Yellow, Green, and Black) Lentils are flavorful, nutritious fillers for soups, salads, and side dishes.

Beans (Navy, Cannellini, Black, Kidney, Butter, Gigante, Lima, Chickpeas) Beans are a staple in my meals, and I like to keep a combination of canned and dried around so I can easily add them to salads, soups, and stews. They are a simple way to add protein to make a filling and complete meal.

SEEDS + NUTS

Seeds and nuts often come to the dairy-free rescue since they are the bases of all of my dairy-free milks, yogurts, and cheeses. They also provide lovely texture and richness to soups, salads, and sauces. Nut and seed butters can transform dressings and sauces, can be used in baked goods, and are great for casual snacking or adding to a smoothie.

Peanuts Technically legumes, peanuts are great for chopping and sprinkling on top of dishes. And, of course, there is peanut butter, which I could not live without.

Almonds (Slivered + Whole) I use whole almonds for nut milk and slivered for topping salads or baked goods.

Almond Butter This is my personal favorite of the nut butters for its sweet almond flavor. It is great in sauces and in smoothies, and can be easily interchanged with peanut butter or most other nut butters.

Walnuts A great addition to sauces such as pesto, walnuts are also nice for sprinkling on top of oatmeal or salads.

Macadamia Nuts I use these sweet, mellow, and rich nuts most often for nut milk, but they are also great for making nut cheese (see the Macadamia Ricotta on page 158).

Cashews I use this nut the most—in nut milk, because it does not require much soaking or any straining, and for creating a rich, creamy, dairy-free cream and yogurt.

Pine Nuts I keep pine nuts stocked so I can make a more traditional pesto in a pinch, but when toasted, they also make a great topper for soup and salads.

Pistachios These have a wonderful sweetness and put a fun twist on nut milk; they are also great in ice cream or sprinkled over chocolaty desserts.

Hazelnuts These nuts are a little more labor-intensive because they need to be toasted and skinned. Toasting brings out their rich nuttiness, which complements anything with chocolate. Hazelnuts also add complexity to soups, such as the Cauliflower Hazelnut Soup with Fried Sage (page 96).

Sesame Seeds Sprinkle them over soups and salad or breakfast porridge, or use them to make Nori Gomasio (page 31).

Tahini This seed butter is best used to make sauces and dressings, such as the Green Herb Tahini (page 38), but I also sneak it into baked goods, such as the Chocolate + Tahini + Sweet Potato Mousse (page 253).

Sunflower Seeds These are a good and nutritious filler seed for sprinkling or for the Apricot + Toasted Coconut Breakfast Bars (page 49).

Pumpkin Seeds Tasty and nutritious, these seeds are great for sprinkling or adding to sauces that call for nuts or seeds, such a pesto.

Hemp Seeds High in omegas, these have a mild grassy flavor and give a nutritional boost to anything you add them to.

HERBS

Fresh herbs are essential for adding flavor, color, and sometimes even health benefits to any dish. Parsley and cilantro, which are often used as garnishes and in sauces, are also known to have detoxifying properties. In addition to using these herbs as a flavor enhancer, I also love to throw in a medley such as mint + basil + cilantro into my smoothies. Most of the herbs listed are ones that I like to grow in my backyard or indoors, so they are always accessible. They are also easy to find at the store and, when stored properly, can be kept for about a week. Alternatively, freeze leftover herbs in ice cube trays with water, and use them in soups, smoothies, or drinks.

• Mint	• Thyme	• Parsley
• Basil	• Sage	• Oregano
• Rosemary	• Cilantro	• Tarragon
• Dill	• Chives	

FROZEN FRUITS, VEGETABLES + SMOOTHIE ADD-INS

Smoothies and drinks are such an important part of my daily food routine that I like to keep a couple of smoothie powders in my pantry to add flavor and a boost of extra nutrients. Sometimes I play around with adding them to baked goods or breakfasts such as oatmeal or cashew yogurt. I also love to keep the freezer stocked with frozen fruits and veggies, not only to easily make a smoothie but also to whip up a meal or side dish.

Spirulina This powerful antioxidant and anti-inflammatory is loaded with nutrients. It has a strong taste, though, so sneak it into a smoothie or nut milk to get its benefits.

Maca Powder Great for balancing hormones, this powder also has a very strong, bitter flavor, so it's best to add to smoothies or warm beverages a teaspoon at a time.

Goji Berries + Powder This bright red antioxidant and anti-inflammatory vitamin-packed powerhouse is wonderful in smoothies, yogurt, and porridges. It has a bitter taste but can complement sweetness. Start with adding a little at a time.

Bee Pollen Just like honey, bee pollen (which too is made by bees) is a highly nutritious food that is loaded with protein and amino acids and is also antibacterial. Add it to smoothies and sprinkle on top of sweet breakfast bowls.

Frozen Fruits and Veggies A variety of frozen berries and veggies can be found in my freezer because they last a long time—and I always have something to add to smoothies, baked fruit dishes, or a veggie stir-fry.

CONDIMENTS

I just love condiments. If you opened my fridge, you would find shelves full of them—many of them homemade and ready to add to any dish. I love condiments so much because I am a big believer that they are the secret weapon for throwing together a delicious meal in no time and making it feel like something special. A jar of homemade romesco has the power to transform baked vegetables into something magical, and a drizzle of shallot vinaigrette can be a pivotal part of a delicious, nourishing salad for lunch.

I often make a condiment when I have an abundance of a certain ingredient that needs to be used up and that could serve as the base of one of my favorite sauces or salad dressings. An overgrowth of basil in the garden quickly translates into pesto by throwing it into the food processor with some garlic, pine nuts, and olive oil. It's then right there in the fridge, ready to add on top of everything from scrambled eggs to a bowl full of veggies and brown rice.

When I don't know what to make for breakfast, lunch, or dinner for myself or for last-minute guests, I'll do what most of us do: open up the fridge and look to see what I have. If I happen to find a homemade condiment or two, I might plan the entire meal around them. Leftover chimichurri would be the perfect accompaniment to a piece of fish. Some green tahini is great for slathering over leftovers and wrapping it all up in a collard wrap or just drizzling it over and tossing it together with some roasted eggplant and a grain. The homemade condiments I share here are staples in my fridge and in my recipes—they are easy to make, are incredibly versatile, and will make your meals more delicious and exciting, while adding layers of flavor and sophistication.

CONDIMENTS

Kale + Olive Pesto   24

Dandelion + Almond Pesto   24

Arugula + Walnut Pesto   24

Roasted Tomato Pesto   25

Tomato + Shallot + Garlic Confit   25

Quick Kale Kimchi   26

Quick Zucchini Kimchi   26

Miso Butter

    Scallion Miso Butter   27

    Nori Miso Butter   27

Quick Pickles   27

Hazelnut or Pumpkin
Seed Dukkah   29

Garlic Chips   30

Crispy Shallots   30

Quinoa "Bread" Crumbs   31

Nori Gomasio   31

Gremolata   31

Chimichurri + Yogurt   32

Carrot Top Harissa   32

Piri Piri Sauce   34

Tarragon Salsa Verde   34

Garlic + Basil Cashew Cream   35

Mint + Pistachio Chutney   35

Mustard Miso   37

Ginger Scallion Sauce   37

Sweet + Spicy Peanut Sauce   37

Easy One-Pan Romesco Sauce   38

Green Herb Tahini   38

Spicy Ginger Sesame Mustard   38

Olive + Basil Tapenade   39

Everyday Shallot +
Mustard Vinaigrette   39

Lemon Caper Vinaigrette   40

Caesar Dressing (Two Ways)

    Classic Caesar Dressing   40

    Vegan Caesar Dressing   41

KALE + OLIVE PESTO

Makes ½ cup of pesto

This pesto has over-the-top flavor thanks to the olives, which add a funky saltiness. It is such a stunner and with robust flavors—it can be eaten over a big bowl of pasta, served over a piece of fish, or even offered as a spread on a charcuterie board.

    10 kale leaves, deribbed

    ¼ cup pitted and chopped olives
    (such as Kalamata)

    1 clove garlic, minced

    Freshly ground black pepper

    Squeeze of lemon juice

    ¼ to ⅓ cup extra virgin olive oil

Bring a large pot of water to a boil. Add the kale to the boiling water and blanch for 2 minutes. Using a slotted spoon or tongs, remove the kale from the boiling water, run it under some cold water, then squeeze to get rid of any excess moisture. Put the kale, olives, garlic, black pepper, and lemon juice in a food processor and pulse a few times until everything is coarsely chopped. Add in the olive oil in a slow stream while the processor is running continuously, until it is emulsified and the pesto is the consistency you desire. Transfer to an airtight container and store in the fridge until use. This will keep for several days in the fridge. Bring to room temperature before serving.

DANDELION + ALMOND PESTO

Makes ½ cup of pesto

Dandelion greens are packed with vitamins and nutrients, and this pesto is a unique and tasty way to enjoy them. There are so many ways to use this pesto, starting with mixing it into a bowl of grains and tossing it with a salad, or simply drizzling it over raw or roasted veggies.

    ⅓ cup almonds

    2 cups loosely packed dandelion greens

    1 small clove garlic, minced

    ¼ teaspoon kosher salt

    Freshly ground black pepper

    ⅓ cup extra virgin olive oil

Put the almonds in a dry frying pan and lightly toast over low heat for a couple of minutes, until lightly browned and fragrant. Put the almonds, dandelion greens, garlic, salt, and black pepper in a food processor and pulse a few times until everything is coarsely chopped. Add in the olive oil in a slow stream while the food processor is running continuously, until emulsified. Transfer to an airtight container and store in the fridge until use. This will keep for several days in the fridge. Bring to room temperature before serving.

ARUGULA + WALNUT PESTO

Makes ¾ cup of pesto

This is a more classical version of pesto and one that I like to make when I have lots of arugula growing in the garden or leftover in the fridge. The pesto goes well with so many things, but one of my favorite uses is to swirl it into a bowl of soup, like the Minestrone with Quinoa and Arugula (page 80).

    ⅓ cup walnuts

    2 cups tightly packed arugula

    1 small clove garlic, minced

    Zest of ½ lemon

    Juice of ½ lemon (about 1 tablespoon)

¼ teaspoon kosher salt

½ cup extra virgin olive oil

Put the walnuts in a dry frying pan and lightly toast over low heat for a couple of minutes, until fragrant. Put the walnuts, arugula, garlic, lemon zest and juice, and salt in a food processor and pulse a few times until everything is coarsely chopped. Add in the olive oil in a slow stream while the food processor is running continuously, until emulsified. Transfer to an airtight container and store in the fridge until use. This will keep for several days in the fridge. Bring to room temperature before serving.

ROASTED TOMATO PESTO

Makes 1 cup of pesto

If tomato sauce and pesto had a really delicious love child, it would be this sauce. Tomato pesto combines all that is wonderful about a traditional basil pesto and adds roasted cherry tomatoes. It's a great sauce that can be simply tossed over pasta or served over toast, but my favorite way to use them is baked with Eggplant Rolls Stuffed with Macadamia Ricotta (page 175).

⅓ cup pine nuts

1 pint cherry tomatoes, halved

⅓ cup extra virgin olive oil + more for drizzling

5 to 7 leaves basil

1 large clove garlic, minced

½ teaspoon kosher salt

Freshly ground black pepper

Pinch of red pepper flakes (optional)

Preheat the oven to 325°F. Put the pine nuts on a small baking sheet and bake for 5 minutes, or until lightly browned and toasted. Transfer to a food processor.

Turn up the oven heat to 400°F. Place a piece of parchment onto the same baking sheet and add the tomatoes and a drizzle of olive oil. Bake for about 30 minutes, until the tomatoes are soft and blistery. Add the tomatoes to the food processor with the pine nuts and allow everything to cool down for about 10 minutes.

Add the basil, garlic, salt, black pepper, and red pepper flakes, if using, and pulse a few times. Add in the olive oil in a slow stream while the food processor is running continuously, until you have a cohesive mixture. Taste, and adjust the seasoning if necessary. Use immediately, or transfer to an airtight container and store in the fridge until use. This will keep for several days in the fridge. Bring to room temperature before serving.

TOMATO + SHALLOT + GARLIC CONFIT

Makes about 4 cups of confit

Summer is such a blissful season. The food, the weather, the beach, the tomatoes—I just want to savor it all for as long as I can. And a jar of this sweet, caramelized tomato goodness is the best way to do that. Roasting tomatoes, shallots, and garlic until they are soft and spreadable is the most delicious way to preserve these summer gems just a little longer. I like to serve this confit with some crusty bread, over greens, or on top of the Chickpea Crepes (page 67).

Special Equipment:
9 x 5-inch loaf pan or small, deep baking dish

1 pint red cherry tomatoes

1 pint Sun Gold (yellow) tomatoes

8 small shallots, peeled and sliced in half

4 cloves garlic, peeled and smashed

6 sprigs fresh thyme

1 teaspoon kosher salt

About 2 cups extra virgin olive oil

Preheat the oven to 350°F. Put the tomatoes, shallots, garlic, thyme, and salt into the pan, and cover with olive oil. Make sure the tomatoes, shallots, and garlic are completely submerged (you may need more or less than the 2 cups). Cover tightly with foil, and bake for about 45 minutes. You want the tomatoes, shallots, and garlic to be tender but not falling apart.

Allow the confit to cool, then transfer to a glass jar with a tight-fitting lid (a large mason jar works great) and serve however you like. The confit will keep in the fridge for a couple of weeks.

QUICK KALE KIMCHI

Makes about 1 cup of kimchi

My dear friend and fellow cookbook author Hetty McKinnon is a vegetable wizard who specializes in high-flavor, high-vibe salads. She makes homemade kimchi for her salads all the time, but I was hesitant to try making my own. What if I messed it up? Hetty assured me that it was easy enough to make it myself at home. Well, she couldn't be more correct—it turns out that kimchi is simple to make and lasts awhile, as long as you don't eat it all right away (this is usually what happens). This recipe is inspired by Hetty's version and is a great gateway into kimichi-ing everything.

1 tablespoon sea salt

6 cups deribbed, roughly chopped kale leaves

½ cup Mushroom Broth (page 110)

2 tablespoons Korean chili powder (see Note)

1 tablespoon apple cider vinegar

2 teaspoons coconut palm sugar

3 cloves garlic

½-inch piece ginger, peeled and roughly chopped

1 shallot, peeled and roughly chopped

Note: If you do not have Korean chili powder on hand (see Resources), you can use any kind of chili powder. I've experimented with different types with excellent results.

In a large bowl, massage the salt into the kale leaves until they wilt and set aside for 30 minutes to 1 hour.

Put the broth, chili powder, vinegar, sugar, garlic, ginger, and shallot into a food processor, and blend until a paste has formed.

After the kale has marinated, rinse it under running water to remove some (but not all) of the salt. Squeeze to release the excess moisture. Add about half of the kimchi paste to the kale and stir to evenly distribute. You can add more paste if you like, or save the remaining paste for another batch of kimchi. Enjoy the kale immediately, or pack tightly into a jar and store in the fridge to enjoy as you please. Kimchi lasts for about 3 months in an airtight jar in the fridge.

QUICK ZUCCHINI KIMCHI

Makes about 1 cup of kimchi

This is a new favorite kimchi of mine, and it is especially great in the summer when the zucchini is plentiful. This is terrific over a burger, with a salad, in a stir-fry, or just on its own.

2 medium zucchini, sliced into rounds

1 tablespoon sea salt

2 tablespoons Korean chili powder (see Note above)

1 tablespoon rice wine vinegar

1 tablespoon toasted sesame oil

2 cloves garlic

½-inch piece ginger, peeled and roughly chopped

1 shallot, peeled and roughly chopped

Put the zucchini and salt in a bowl, and toss to combine. Set aside for 30 minutes to 1 hour. Rinse under running water to remove some (but not all) of the salt. Squeeze to release any excess moisture, and set aside on a paper towel to allow the extra moisture to be absorbed while you make the paste.

Put the chili powder, vinegar, sesame oil, garlic, ginger, and shallot into a food processor and pulse until you have a thick paste. Put the zucchini back into the bowl and toss with the paste. Serve immediately or pack into a glass jar with a tight-fitting lid to enjoy later. Kimchi lasts for about 3 months in an airtight jar in the fridge.

MISO BUTTER

Makes ¼ cup miso butter

Miso butter is the greatest thing to happen to both miso and butter. It is a flavor bomb that explodes when tossed with anything, but especially with vegetables. It is so good, I often make a double batch and just keep it in the fridge so it is always ready, especially for a quick and casual weeknight meal.

Scallion Miso Butter

The addition of scallions to basic miso butter gives it an extra punch of both flavor and color, which makes it an ideal way to finish roasted vegetables.

4 teaspoons white miso

4 tablespoons unsalted butter, softened at room temperature

2 scallions, white and light green parts only, sliced

In a small bowl, mix together the miso and butter with a fork, then fold in the scallions. To store, roll it into a log using parchment paper, trim any excess off the edges of the parchment, and wrap it tightly in plastic wrap. Store in the fridge until ready to use. This will keep for a couple of weeks in the fridge.

Nori Miso Butter

This miso butter gets a double umami boost from the mineral-packed seaweed nori. It is great as a finisher to the Crisp Sautéed Maitake Mushrooms on page 188, or you could also smear this over toast and top with roasted mushrooms or veggies.

Special Equipment:
Mortar and pestle or spice grinder

1 sheet toasted nori

4 teaspoons white miso

4 tablespoons unsalted butter, softened at room temperature

Grind the nori with a mortar and pestle (or in a spice grinder) until fine. In a small bowl, mix the nori, miso, and butter together with a fork until combined. To store, roll it into a log using parchment paper, trim any excess off the edges of the parchment, and wrap it tightly in plastic wrap. Store in the fridge until ready to use. This will keep for several weeks in the fridge.

QUICK PICKLES

Makes about 1 cup of pickled veggies

Quick pickles are an easy way to add a flavorful punch to salads, sandwiches, roasted veggies, or tacos. You can follow this simple formula to quick pickle anything, and you get to eat them just 30 minutes later. Alternatively, you can store your quick pickles in an airtight jar in the fridge

and enjoy them for weeks. Feel free to play around with different herbs or spices added to the brine to give layers of flavor.

> 1 cup vegetable for pickling (see below)
>
> 1 cup water
>
> ½ cup apple cider vinegar
>
> 2 tablespoons white granulated sugar
>
> 1 tablespoon kosher salt
>
> Add-ins (optional; see below)

SOME OF MY FAVORITE THINGS TO PICKLE:

- Chilies + Cumin seed
- Cucumber + Fennel seed
- Fennel + Mustard seed
- Okra + Garlic
- Peppers + Chili flakes
- Radishes + Pink peppercorns
- Red onion + Black peppercorns
- Zucchini + Coriander

Optional add-ins:

- 1 tablespoon peppercorns
- 1 teaspoon mustard, cumin, or fennel seeds
- 1 bay leaf
- Fresh herbs (such as dill or cilantro)

Slice the vegetables as you wish, and pack them into a mason jar with a tight-fitting lid. Put the water, vinegar, sugar, salt, and any other add-ins, if using, into a medium saucepan. Bring to a boil, remove from the heat, and allow the liquid to cool for about 10 minutes, then pour the liquid over the vegetables. Allow to cool to room temperature before serving, or before covering and storing in the fridge. These will keep for about 1 month in the fridge.

HAZELNUT OR PUMPKIN SEED DUKKAH

Makes 1 cup of dukkah

Dukkah, an Egyptian spice blend, is a relatively new addition to my spice shelf but a welcome one for its unique flavor and versatility. Some of the best uses for this delicious blend include sprinkling it on oats for breakfast or over roasted veggies for dinner. It is also a great addition to croutons (Dukkah, Pine Nut + Oat Croutons, page 118).

> ½ cup hazelnuts or pumpkin seeds
>
> ¼ cup sesame seeds
>
> 2 tablespoons coriander seeds
>
> 2 tablespoons cumin seeds
>
> 1 teaspoon dried thyme
>
> 1 teaspoon black peppercorns
>
> ½ teaspoon fennel seeds
>
> ½ teaspoon sea salt
>
> 1 teaspoon sumac (optional)

If you are using hazelnuts, preheat the oven to 350°F. Place the hazelnuts on a baking sheet and bake for 10 to 15 minutes, until they are lightly browned and fragrant, and the skins are starting to come off. Allow them to cool slightly, then separate the skins by rubbing the hazelnuts with a towel. Put the peeled hazelnuts in a food processor.

In a dry cast iron pan over medium heat, toast the pumpkin seeds, if using, and the sesame seeds for a couple of minutes, until lightly browned. Keep your eye on them, because this happens very quickly. Remove the seeds and put them in a food processor. In the same pan, add the coriander, cumin, thyme, peppercorns, and fennel, and toast for about 2 minutes, until fragrant. Add them to the food processor.

Add the salt and sumac, if using, to the food processor, and pulse several times until the mix is fine and somewhat evenly textured. This will keep in an airtight container on the countertop for several weeks.

GARLIC CHIPS
Makes about ¼ cup of garlic chips

If you love garlic as much as I do, then these crunchy, flavorful garlic chips will be your new best friend. The garlicky bits are a simple way to elevate meals, particularly soups or salads. The Parsnip Chowder (page 104) is a good place to start sprinkling these power-packed chips.

> **Special Equipment:**
> Mandoline
>
> 4 tablespoons grapeseed or peanut oil
>
> 10 to 12 cloves very fresh garlic, thinly sliced with a mandoline

Line a plate with paper towels. Put the grapeseed oil in a small saucepan and place it on the burner, but do not turn the heat on yet. Have a small fine-mesh strainer or slotted spoon nearby.

Put the garlic in a medium saucepan with about 1 inch of cold water. Bring it to a boil, then remove it from the heat and scoop out the garlic using the slotted spoon and rest it on the plate.

Heat the saucepan with the grapeseed oil over medium-high heat. When the oil is hot enough (it will start to look wavy on the surface), add the garlic and give it a shake to make sure the slices don't stick together. Cook the garlic until it just starts to brown (this will happen quickly); be sure you don't overcook or else the chips will taste bitter. Remove the garlic from the oil using the slotted spoon and place them on the paper towel–lined plate. Once cooled, store in an airtight container until you're ready to use.

These will last for about 2 weeks in an airtight container in the fridge.

CRISPY SHALLOTS
Makes about ¼ cup of crispy shallots

Crispy shallots are another wonderful crunchy topping, because they are easy to make and bring a super flavorful crunch to anything you add them to. Salads and sandwiches are perfect for these crispy shallots, but the ultimate use for these is as a soup topper. The Curried Sweet Potato + Yellow Split Pea Stew (page 99) is a great match for these crispy bits.

> 3 tablespoons chickpea flour
>
> Sea salt
>
> Freshly ground black pepper
>
> 1 large shallot, thinly sliced
>
> 3 tablespoons grapeseed oil (or other high-heat oil)

On a large plate, mix the flour with a pinch of salt and pepper. Add the shallot to the flour mixture and toss to coat.

Line a small plate with paper towels and have it nearby. In a small frying pan, heat the oil over medium-high heat. Test to make sure the oil is hot enough by adding a shallot; if it sizzles, it's ready. Add the remaining shallots and cook for 3 to 4 minutes, shaking the pan occasionally (but try not to disturb the shallots too much). Do this until they start to brown, but be careful because they quickly turn from light brown to burnt. Using a slotted spoon, transfer the shallots to the plate with the paper towel. Use right away, or store in the fridge. They will keep for about 2 weeks in an airtight container in the fridge.

QUINOA "BREAD" CRUMBS

Makes 1 cup bread crumbs

When looking for gluten-free bread crumbs, I found that the store-bought options were always highly processed, so I decided to make them at home using my favorite gluten-free grain as a substitute. It turns out that quinoa, when crisped up in the oven and with a few spices added to it, makes a great gluten-free bread crumb! The best way to make this is using leftover quinoa sitting in the fridge—the cooler and drier the quinoa is, the more crisp the crumb will be. If you're using leftover quinoa, skip to the step where you spread the quinoa onto the baking sheet and bake it in the oven.

½ cup quinoa, rinsed well

1 cup water

¼ teaspoon sea salt

Pinch of dried parsley

Pinch of red pepper flakes

Pinch of garlic powder

Freshly ground black pepper

Add the quinoa and water to a small saucepan. Bring to a boil, cover, reduce to a simmer, and cook for 15 minutes. When the quinoa is done, spread it out on a baking sheet and place it in the fridge for about 30 minutes to cool before toasting.

Preheat the oven to 350°F. Make sure the quinoa is in one thin, even layer spread across the baking sheet. This is important, because it will ensure it will toast evenly. Place the quinoa in the oven for 20 to 30 minutes, until it turns golden brown. Check after 20 minutes, and if it is not yet golden brown, keep checking back every 5 minutes because this will happen quickly. Put the toasted quinoa into a food processor and add the salt, parsley, red pepper flakes, garlic powder, and black pepper to taste. Run the food processor until you have a fine textured crumb. This will keep in an airtight jar on the countertop for a couple of weeks.

NORI GOMASIO

Makes a little more than 1 cup of gomasio

Gomasio is a Japanese condiment made up of sesame seeds and salt, and I like to think of it as a more nutritious finishing salt. I often add some nori to my gomasio, which ups the nutritional value and gives it a boost of iodine, a nutrient we all need. I sprinkle this over anything and everything, from soup to salad to roasted vegetables and even over my oatmeal for breakfast.

1 cup sesame seeds

1 tablespoon sea salt

1 sheet toasted nori, coarsely chopped

Heat a medium frying pan over low heat, and add the sesame seeds. Cook for 3 to 5 minutes, until golden brown. Transfer the seeds to a food processor along with the sea salt and nori, and pulse just a few times until the mixture is uniform in size (tiny granules), but be careful not to overprocess as you still want texture to the sesame seeds. This gomasio will last for several months in an airtight jar in the pantry.

GREMOLATA

Makes ¼ cup of gremolata

Gremolata is an Italian condiment made up of garlic, lemon, and herbs and is traditionally served over meat. I love gremolata because it is a little flavor bomb that adds a nice punch, but I like to throw mine over vegetables instead of meat, such as the Garlic + Lemon Marinated Artichokes (page 172).

Special Equipment:
Microplane

Small handful of parsley, minced

1 large clove garlic

Zest of 1 lemon

Put the minced parsley in a small bowl. Using a Microplane, grate the garlic clove over the parsley, and mince the remaining garlic that gets too small to grate. Zest the lemon over the parsley and garlic, and give it a stir to combine. Use immediately.

CHIMICHURRI + YOGURT

Makes ¾ cup of chimichurri

My husband, Michael, is the chimichurri maker in our house. He makes the best chimichurri I have ever had, and is very particular about the ingredients he uses, as well as the amount of time it marinates (the longer it sits, the better it is). This is his "secret" chimichurri recipe, and even though it is traditionally served with steak, we love to use it on chicken, fish, vegetables, and scrambled eggs in the morning. There is an option here to add yogurt to the chimichurri, which I like to do sometimes when I am serving it over a veggie burger or as a dip with vegetables.

　　1 cup loosely packed cilantro

　　1 cup loosely packed parsley

　　⅓ cup diced red onion

　　4 cloves garlic

　　½ jalapeño pepper, deseeded

　　½ cup extra virgin olive oil

　　3 tablespoons red wine vinegar

　　½ teaspoon kosher salt

　　6 ounces plain Greek (or coconut, sheep's, or goat's milk) yogurt (optional)

Note: It's best to make this a day or two before you use it, so the flavors develop. Make it no less than 30 minutes before serving.

Separately chop the cilantro, parsley, onion, garlic, and jalapeño, then add them to one large pile on the cutting board and continue to chop them all together until the ingredients are minced and uniform in size. Transfer them to a small bowl, and add the olive oil, vinegar, and salt, and stir. Cover, and set it aside for about 30 minutes or until you're ready to serve. Store in the fridge in an airtight container. If you are using the yogurt, stir it in right before you're ready to serve.

CARROT TOP HARISSA

Makes ¾ cup of harissa

Beautiful carrot top greens often get thrown away, but they are actually incredibly tasty and are perfect for garnishing or making sauces. They remind me of parsley but with a more mellow taste. While you can use carrot tops where any herbs are called for (especially parsley), their fresh, grassy but subtle flavor works perfectly in this delicious herb-packed harissa.

　　1 cup loosely packed green carrot tops

　　½ cup loosely packed cilantro

　　3 to 4 mint leaves

　　1 small clove garlic, minced

　　Juice of ½ lemon

　　½ teaspoon ground cumin

　　½ teaspoon ground coriander

　　¼ teaspoon sea salt

　　½ cup extra virgin olive oil

Put the carrot tops, cilantro, mint, garlic, lemon, cumin, coriander, and salt into a food processor and pulse a few times. Add in the olive oil in a slow stream while the processor is running continuously, until you have a consistent mixture. Store in an airtight container in the fridge when not in use. This will keep for a few days in the fridge.

PIRI PIRI SAUCE

Makes a little more than 1 cup of sauce

A more traditional piri piri sauce, which is African and Portuguese in origin, is typically paired with chicken or shrimp. I am so in love with this simple, spicy, flavorful sauce that I was inspired to come up with a version of my own. Since it is hard to find piri piri peppers (used in the traditional recipe), I just use whatever red chili I can find—typically a serrano or Thai chili. Just keep in mind how spicy (or mild) you want the sauce to be. This version has a serious kick, so if you love heat, there are so many things you will want to slather it all over.

¼ cup extra virgin olive oil

1 small red onion, thinly sliced

1 red bell pepper, thinly sliced

2 mild to medium red chilies, deseeded and thinly sliced

½ teaspoon sea salt

3 cloves garlic, minced

1 teaspoon paprika

Juice of ½ lemon (about 1 tablespoon)

1 tablespoon chopped parsley

Heat the olive oil in a large cast iron pan over medium heat. Add the onion, pepper, and chilies, and cook for 10 to 12 minutes, until the vegetables are soft and starting to brown. Add the salt, garlic, and paprika and cook for another

2 minutes. Transfer the mixture to a food processor, add the lemon juice and parsley, and blend until smooth. Use right away or keep in an airtight container in the fridge for up to 1 week.

TARRAGON SALSA VERDE

Makes about 1 cup of salsa

Salsa verde, which you might think of as simply green salsa, is so much more than that. Salsa verde is what convinced me that anchovies deserve a place in my pantry as well as in my sauces. This sauce packs so much flavor, you can use it on everything from eggs to a simple grilled whole fish. If anchovies are not your thing, you can leave them out and use capers instead. Also, feel free to change out the tarragon for basil or cilantro if the mood strikes.

6 anchovy fillets or 2 tablespoons capers

1 clove garlic, minced

2 tablespoons minced parsley

1 tablespoon minced tarragon

2 pinches lemon zest

Juice of ½ lemon (about 1 tablespoon)

Sea salt

Freshly ground black pepper

Pinch of red pepper flakes

1 tablespoon white wine vinegar

½ to ⅔ cup extra virgin olive oil

Put the anchovies and garlic on a cutting board, and chop until you have a very fine paste. Add in the parsley and tarragon, and chop until the herbs are incorporated. Put the chopped mixture into a small bowl and add the lemon zest and juice, a pinch or two of salt, black pepper, red pepper flakes, and the white wine vinegar. Add in the olive oil while whisking, until you have the desired consistency. I find that a little more than ½ cup makes the perfect consistency. Use right away, or store in an airtight container in the fridge for later use. This salsa will keep for about 1 week in the fridge.

GARLIC + BASIL CASHEW CREAM

Makes 1 cup of cashew cream

Cashew cream is the best way to get a dairy-like consistency without the dairy. And when you add delicious things to it such as garlic and basil, you forget all about those cashews. Feel free to experiment by adding other flavors or spices to this cashew cream base. You could easily add in or swap out additional herbs such as parsley and cilantro. You could also leave out the herbs altogether and just play around with cumin or paprika or other spices.

½ cup cashews

¼ cup water

1 clove garlic

10 basil leaves

¼ teaspoon kosher salt

1 teaspoon apple cider vinegar

Juice of ½ lemon
(about 1 tablespoon)

Soak the cashews for about 3 hours, or overnight. Drain and put the soaked cashews into a food processor with the water and process until smooth (add a little more water, a tablespoon at a time, if it is too thick). Add the garlic, basil, salt, vinegar, and lemon juice and pulse several times until all the ingredients are incorporated. This will keep for a couple of days in the fridge.

MINT + PISTACHIO CHUTNEY

Makes about ½ cup of chutney

There is a place near my home that makes dosas, delicious Indian crepes made from a batter of fermented lentils and rice, and typically served with a side of chutney. I always have a hard time deciding which kind of chutney to order because they are all so tasty. Inspired by these incredible chutneys, I started making my own at home and was surprised at how easily they came together. There are so many different flavor combinations you could experiment with, but this mint and pistachio combo is particularly good—especially for dipping and spreading.

¼ cup shelled pistachios

½ teaspoon coriander seeds

1½ cups loosely packed mint

1 clove garlic

¼ cup diced shallots

½ teaspoon lemon zest

1 small, mild green chili, deseeded

½ teaspoon sea salt

2 to 3 tablespoons grapeseed oil
(or any neutral oil)

Toast the pistachios and coriander seeds lightly in a small dry pan over low heat, for about 2 minutes, until fragrant. Put the toasted pistachios and coriander in a food processor along with the mint, garlic, shallots, lemon zest, chili, salt, and grapeseed oil. Pulse several times until a thick paste has formed (I like to keep some chunks for texture). Transfer to a small dish and set aside until you're ready to serve. You can also do this a day or so in advance (it would actually be better since the flavors will have time to develop). You can also add a little

more (neutral) oil, if you like, which makes it a bit smoother for dipping. This will keep for several days in the fridge.

MUSTARD MISO

Makes ⅓ cup of mustard miso

Mustard and miso are a tasty pair, and this sauce is so versatile—it can be used for dressing, dipping, and marinating. Sometimes I make this as a dip for raw vegetables or a spread for collard wraps (page 162), but one of my favorite uses for this sauce is as a marinade for any kind of white fish.

> 2 tablespoons Dijon mustard
>
> 1 teaspoon white miso
>
> 2 teaspoons apple cider vinegar
>
> 1 teaspoon tamari
>
> 1 teaspoon toasted sesame oil
>
> 2 to 3 tablespoons water

Whisk all the ingredients together in a small bowl. Serve immediately. This will keep for a couple of weeks in an airtight container in the fridge.

GINGER SCALLION SAUCE

Makes ⅓ cup of sauce

Ginger and scallions are a classic duo, and with just a few other additions such as lime juice and sesame oil, you have an addictive sauce that you will want to serve on top of everything. This pairs well with so many dishes, but I think it is best over the Crispy Cauliflower Steaks (page 180).

> 6 scallions, white and light green parts only, thinly sliced
>
> 1 jalapeño or mild green chili, deseeded and thinly sliced
>
> 1 teaspoon grated ginger

> 1 tablespoon freshly squeezed lime juice
>
> 1 teaspoon toasted sesame oil
>
> 1 teaspoon honey
>
> Kosher salt

Whisk together all the ingredients in a small bowl. Serve immediately. This will keep for a couple of days in an airtight container in the fridge.

SWEET + SPICY PEANUT SAUCE

Makes about ½ cup of sauce

A classic peanut sauce is delicious and has so many uses beyond noodles. This sauce pairs particularly well with sweet potatoes, so I use it over Thai Peanut Sweet Potato Skins (page 154) as well as over the raw Cucumber Noodle Pad Thai (page 125).

> ¼ cup peanut or almond butter
>
> 2 tablespoons tamari or coconut aminos
>
> 2 tablespoons brown rice vinegar
>
> 1 tablespoon freshly squeezed lime juice
>
> Dash or two of hot sauce
>
> 1 thumbnail-size piece ginger
>
> 1 small clove garlic, minced
>
> 2 teaspoons honey
>
> 1 teaspoon toasted sesame oil
>
> About 2 tablespoons water

Put the peanut butter, tamari, vinegar, lime juice, hot sauce, ginger, garlic, honey, and sesame oil into a food processor and run continuously until smooth. Add the water, or just enough that the mixture will coat the back of a spoon. Serve immediately. This will keep for about a week in an airtight container in the fridge.

EASY ONE-PAN ROMESCO SAUCE

Makes 1½ cups of romesco

Romesco is a roasted tomato and pepper sauce that is blended together with nuts, garlic, vinegar, and a few other seasonings. A traditional romesco has bread and is a little more labor-intensive than this simplified version, which is free of the bread and also allows you to cook everything in one pan before transferring it to the food processor. I particularly like this over grilled alliums such as leeks or scallions, but I also love to serve it over sautéed Romano or green beans.

½ cup sliced almonds

2 cloves garlic, peels left on

2 red peppers, sliced

2 plum tomatoes, halved

1 dried chipotle pepper, soaked and deseeded

½ teaspoon kosher salt

Freshly ground black pepper

1 tablespoon sherry vinegar

½ cup extra virgin olive oil

Preheat the oven to 325°F. Place the almonds and garlic on a baking sheet and bake for 10 minutes, or until the almonds are lightly toasted. Remove the garlic from the sheet, peel, and put the garlic and nuts in a food processor.

Turn up the oven heat to 450°F. Place the peppers and tomatoes on the baking sheet and roast for about 25 minutes, until the edges are starting to char. Remove and put them in the food processor. Add the chipotle pepper, salt, black pepper, vinegar, and olive oil into the food processor and blend until super-smooth. Taste and adjust the seasoning as necessary. This will keep for a couple of days in an airtight container in the fridge.

GREEN HERB TAHINI

Makes about ½ cup tahini

I am so in love with this tahini. It is great to make when you have lots of leftover herbs in the fridge or an abundance in the garden. It is super-versatile, and the flavors of the herbs and lemon play so nicely with the nuttiness of the tahini. It can be tossed with vegetables or noodles, or served as a dressing with any salad, but I also imagine it would be great over a veggie burger or alongside a veggie fritter. Because I rely on this dressing so much, you will see it several times throughout the book.

¼ cup loosely packed parsley

¼ cup loosely packed cilantro

7 basil leaves

3 tablespoons tahini

1 clove garlic

Juice of ½ lemon (about 1 tablespoon)

½ teaspoon sea salt

⅓ cup extra virgin olive oil

Put the parsley, cilantro, basil, tahini, garlic, lemon juice, and salt in the food processor. Pulse a couple of times, then add in the olive oil in a slow steam while the food processor is running continuously, scraping down the sides as needed. Feel free to add a tablespoon or two of water to thin it out. Use immediately, or transfer to an airtight container for later use. This should keep for about 1 week in the fridge.

SPICY GINGER SESAME MUSTARD

Makes about ¼ cup mustard

This spicy ginger mustard is a must in my fridge. While I usually serve it over fish, such as salmon, I also whip this up to toss with salad greens, rice noodles, or anytime I am craving those spicy, mustard, gingery, sesame flavors.

> ½-inch piece ginger, grated
>
> 1 clove garlic, minced
>
> 1 tablespoon grapeseed oil (or other neutral oil)
>
> 1 teaspoon toasted sesame oil
>
> Juice of 1 lemon (about 2 tablespoons)
>
> 2 teaspoons Dijon mustard
>
> ¼ teaspoon sea salt
>
> Freshly ground black pepper

Whisk all the ingredients together in a small bowl. Store in an airtight container in the fridge when not in use. This will keep for about a week in the fridge.

OLIVE + BASIL TAPENADE

Makes 1½ cups of tapenade

Olive tapenade is a classic mixture of olives, garlic, and herbs. Since I just adore olives, I like to use this as either a sauce or a dip when I am craving those salty olive flavors. I also like to make this when I have leftover olives from a party—I just quickly chop them up for the tapenade and serve it with some toast or over a piece of fish.

> ½ cup pitted and coarsely chopped green olives
>
> ½ cup pitted and coarsely chopped purple olives (such as Kalamata)
>
> 5 basil leaves, coarsely chopped
>
> 2 cloves garlic, minced
>
> Pinch or two of red pepper flakes
>
> Juice of ½ lemon (about 1 tablespoon)
>
> ¼ cup extra-virgin olive oil

Put the olives, basil, garlic, and red pepper on a cutting board, mix them together, and chop a few more times until everything is incorporated. Transfer the olive mixture to a small bowl and add the lemon juice and olive oil and stir to combine. Serve immediately. This will keep for a few days in an airtight container in the fridge.

EVERYDAY SHALLOT + MUSTARD VINAIGRETTE

Makes about 1 cup of vinaigrette

This is hands down my go-to salad dressing. I almost always have this in my fridge in a mason jar, ready to go. I make it often when I am having guests—people always ask what's in the dressing and are surprised to hear that it is a pretty simple and standard French vinaigrette. The ingredient that gives the dressing its zing and makes it stand out is a good-quality sherry vinegar. I would highly recommend finding a sherry vinegar that you love and always keeping it in your pantry, since it makes so many things, including this dressing, taste so, so good.

> 2 tablespoons minced shallots
>
> 2 tablespoons sherry vinegar
>
> 2 teaspoons Dijon mustard
>
> ½ teaspoon kosher salt
>
> Freshly ground black pepper
>
> ⅓ cup extra virgin olive oil

Put the shallots, vinegar, mustard, salt, and pepper to taste into a food processor and pulse a few times to chop. Scrape down the sides. Add in the olive oil in a slow stream while the food processor is running continuously. Taste, and adjust the amount of oil and any seasoning as necessary. (You want the dressing to be on the tart/acidic side, because it will mellow out once it coats the greens.) I like to store this in a mason jar with a tight-fitting lid in the fridge, and then when I want to use it, I take it out and shake it up. It will keep for several days in the fridge.

LEMON CAPER VINAIGRETTE

Makes ½ cup of vinaigrette

This is a simple, classic vinaigrette that goes perfectly with any grilled or baked white fish, thanks to the bright tartness from the lemon and the salty finish of the capers. As with most vinaigrettes, it would also be lovely over simple salad greens.

1 tablespoon rinsed capers, minced

1 tablespoon minced shallots

1 clove garlic, minced

½ teaspoon Dijon mustard

½ teaspoon whole grain mustard

Juice of 1 lemon (about 2 tablespoons)

1 tablespoon chopped parsley

Sea salt

Freshly ground black pepper

¼ cup extra virgin olive oil

Put the capers, shallots, garlic, mustards, lemon juice, parsley, a pinch or two of salt, and pepper to taste in a small mixing bowl, and whisk in the olive oil in a slow stream. Allow to sit for 30 minutes before serving to allow the flavors to develop. This will keep for about 1 week in an airtight container in the fridge.

CAESAR DRESSING (TWO WAYS)

I love a perfect Caesar dressing, preferably homemade—raw egg, anchovies, and all. A classic Caesar has lots of cheese added to the dressing, but I make mine without and I don't miss it one bit. It's every bit as tangy and wonderful without cheese. I am also sharing my recipe for an eggless and anchovyless (vegan) Caesar—it is a wonderful spin on the classic dressing, and I use it all the time. It's a great option if you (or someone you're serving it to) have an aversion or allergy to any of the ingredients in a traditional Caesar dressing.

Classic Caesar Dressing

Makes about ½ cup of dressing

1 small clove garlic

2 anchovies

½ teaspoon Dijon mustard

Juice of ½ lemon (about 1 tablespoon)

Sea salt

Freshly ground black pepper

1 egg yolk

¼ cup extra virgin olive oil

Put the garlic and anchovies on a cutting board, and mince together until a paste has formed. Put the mixture in a small mixing bowl with the mustard, lemon juice, pinch of salt, pepper to taste, and egg yolk, and whisk. While whisking continuously, add in the olive oil in a slow stream until the dressing is creamy and emulsified. Keep in the fridge in an airtight container when not in use. This is best to use within the same day but will still be okay to use in a couple of days if kept in an airtight jar in the fridge.

Vegan Caesar Dressing

Makes about ¾ cup of dressing

- ¼ cup extra virgin olive oil

- ⅓ cup vegan mayonnaise
  or regular mayonnaise

- Juice of ½ lemon
  (about 1 tablespoon)

- 1 teaspoon Dijon mustard

- 1 teaspoon vegan or nonvegan
  Worcestershire sauce

- 1 clove garlic, minced

- 1 teaspoon apple cider vinegar

- ½ teaspoon sea salt

- Freshly ground black pepper

Put all the ingredients in a small mixing bowl, and whisk to combine. Use immediately, or transfer to an airtight container and store in the fridge. This will keep for a couple of days in the fridge.

BREAKFAST

My mornings are the one time of day when I enjoy sticking to a strict routine. The early morning is usually when I feel like I can have a little peace, especially on weekdays, before the mad rush of emails and dishes start piling up. My morning routine always includes a walk with the dog around the neighborhood, a few minutes of meditation, and a warm beverage. Then, there's breakfast.

Breakfast for me falls into two categories: a quick weekday breakfast, or a leisurely weekend breakfast. There are times when breakfast needs to be fast, with little effort, so I can get on with my day. I do believe that a healthy breakfast is that much more important when you are busy, so for those kinds of mornings, colorful smoothies and warming bowls of oatmeal are usually my go-tos—I get the most amount of nourishment with the least amount of effort. Weekends and days off are much more relaxed. When there isn't much more on the agenda besides reading the paper, walking on the beach, or watching a movie, we like to linger in the kitchen, make the morning last as long as possible, and get more creative with breakfast. We introduce eggs from the farm into the rotation, sometimes baked, sometimes scrambled. A close second, when we are feeling extra decadent, would be pancakes or waffles, piled high with fresh fruit and topped with a blanket of maple syrup. Here are some of my favorite breakfasts—the quick and easy weekday staples and the weekend treats.

BREAKFAST

Coconut + Cherry + Oatmeal Soufflé   46

Apricot + Toasted Coconut
Breakfast Bars   49

Easy Cashew "Yogurt" Parfait   50

Coconut + Ginger + Turmeric Oats   53

Smoothies   54

Blueberry Bottom Buckwheat
with Tahini + Maple + Cashew Milk   59

Miso Oats with Scallions +
Sesame Oil   60

Banana + Oat + Cardamom
Pancakes   63

Sweet Potato + Chickpea +
Poblano Hash with a Fried Egg   64

Chickpea Crepes (Three Ways)

   Basic Chickpea Crepe
   + Smashed Avocado   67

   Cumin + Jalapeño Crepe with
   Tomato + Cucumber Salad   68

   Paprika Chili Crepe + Soft
   Scrambled Eggs with Chives   68

Cauliflower "Grits" with Crispy
Shittakes + Spinach   69

Milks   70

Caraway Tomato Baked Eggs   73

Homemade Puffed Rice Cereal   74

COCONUT + CHERRY + OATMEAL SOUFFLÉ

Special Equipment:
9 x 7-inch or 8 x 8-inch baking dish

16 ounces (2 cups) frozen cherries

1 cup rolled oats

½ teaspoon baking powder

Sea salt

1 cup full-fat coconut milk

¼ cup water

1 egg

½ teaspoon vanilla extract

Sprinkle of shaved coconut

Although I tend to be more of a savory breakfast person, occasionally I do crave a breakfast that feels like dessert. This breakfast is super-simple to make, and better yet, it is made with staple pantry ingredients (as long as you have some frozen fruit in the freezer). The flavor combination of coconut and cherry is delightful; however, if you do not happen to have frozen cherries on hand, blueberries, strawberries, or even mango could be used instead.

———————

Preheat the oven to 375°F. Pour the cherries into the baking dish. In a medium bowl, mix together the oats, baking powder, and a pinch of salt. In a separate bowl, mix together the coconut milk and water. In a small bowl, lightly beat the egg and mix together the coconut milk/water mixture and vanilla. Pour the dry ingredients over the cherries, then pour the wet mixture evenly over top. Finish with the shaved coconut.

Bake for 30 minutes, or until bubbly and lightly browned. Allow to cool for about 10 minutes before serving. Serve warm.

APRICOT + TOASTED COCONUT
BREAKFAST BARS

Special Equipment:
8 x 8-inch baking dish

2 cups shaved coconut

½ cup sesame seeds

½ cup sunflower seeds

1½ cups rolled oats

½ cup chopped dried apricots

½ cup brown rice syrup or honey

Sea salt

There are mornings when a grab-and-go breakfast is totally necessary, so I keep a few things around, in either the fridge or freezer, for when the need strikes. This is my main breakfast bar recipe. The thing I love most about this recipe is that it is forgiving—the dried fruit, seeds, and nuts can be interchanged for what you have on hand or depending on what kind of mood you're in. Feel free to play around with different variations keeping these ratios in mind. Dried blueberries, cherries, or dates could replace the apricots, and you can use one cup of a nut (such as almonds) in place of the sunflower and sesame seeds.

Line the baking dish with parchment and set aside.

Put the coconut, sesame seeds, and sunflower seeds in a dry frying pan and toast over low heat until the coconut is lightly browned and fragrant, about 2 to 3 minutes. Transfer to a large mixing bowl and add in the oats, apricots, brown rice syrup, and a pinch of salt and stir until all of the ingredients are incorporated. Transfer the mixture to the baking dish, and using wet fingers (this will keep the mixture from sticking to you), press it evenly into the dish. Cover and cool in the fridge for 3 hours before you slice into bars.

I like to wrap these individually in parchment, and keep them in an airtight container in the fridge, so I can grab them on the run. These will keep for a couple of weeks in the fridge.

EASY CASHEW "YOGURT" PARFAIT

Yogurt

2 cups cashews

1 ripe banana

1 teaspoon vanilla

1 tablespoon coconut oil

Sea salt

2 tablespoons freshly squeezed orange juice

1 probiotic capsule

½ to ⅔ cup water

Parfait

1 cup fresh or frozen berries (such as blueberries, raspberries, or blackberries)

½ cup granola

Bee pollen (optional)

Chia or hemp seeds (optional)

I make this cashew "yogurt" often because it is so easy, and one big batch will last for a few breakfasts. The probiotics help with digestion while giving it that tangy yogurt taste; however, if you don't have a probiotic capsule on hand, you can simply leave it out. If you don't love banana, or want to play around with other flavors, feel free to add a half cup of the fruit of your choice. Dates, raspberries, or blueberries would all work well to flavor the yogurt, but keep in mind the color of the fruit will change the color of the yogurt.

Yogurt

Soak the cashews for 3 hours or overnight. Drain and put them in a high-powered blender or food processor. Add the banana, vanilla, coconut oil, a pinch of salt, and orange juice, and empty in the contents of the probiotic capsule. While the blender or food processor is running continuously, add ½ cup of the water in a slow stream. You might need a little more than a ½ cup; if so, add additional water a tablespoon at a time, until the mixture runs smooth but is still thick and creamy. Put in the fridge for 30 minutes, and your "yogurt" is ready to enjoy. It is even better after the probiotic has a day or two to work its magic.

Parfait

Layer the fruit, granola, and bee pollen or seeds, if using, alternating with layers of yogurt. I like to do this in small mason jars with tight-fitting lids and store them in the fridge. These will keep for a few days in an airtight container in the fridge.

COCONUT + GINGER + TURMERIC OATS

Special Equipment:
Microplane

One 13½-ounce can light or full-fat coconut milk, or 1½ cups other nondairy milk (such as almond or cashew milk; page 70)

1-inch piece turmeric, peeled

1-inch piece ginger, peeled

1 tablespoon honey

Sea salt

1 cup quick-cooking rolled oats

Cinnamon, to finish

There is a cute café several blocks from our house where I usually end up after a long walk with our dog. They serve the most delicious turmeric oats as a special dish, and they inspired me to create my own version at home. These oats are basically a marriage of oatmeal and golden milk. The ginger gives the oats a beautiful warming flavor, and turmeric is to thank for its vibrant, creamy yellow hue. If you do not have fresh turmeric on hand, you can sub one teaspoon of ground instead.

———————

Put the coconut milk in a medium saucepan over low heat. Grate both the turmeric and ginger into the coconut milk using a Microplane or a fine grater. Add the honey and salt, and stir until the honey has dissolved. Add the oats, and cook while stirring often until the oats are the consistency you like. I prefer mine a little on the wet side, so I cook them for a shorter amount of time. Spoon into individual bowls, and finish with a sprinkle of cinnamon.

SMOOTHIES

Smoothies are a quick and tasty way to nourish yourself. The kind of smoothie I make often depends on my mood, the season, or the time of day. In the summer I prefer bright, refreshing smoothies with fruits like pineapple and strawberries. In the winter I nix the ice and go for warming smoothies with mix-ins like cooked rolled oats and ginger. Smoothies are a great way to make sure you're getting a colorful array of fruits and vegetables in your diet, so the following is a list of some of my most-used ingredients, by color. You can mix and match them depending on your craving or the season, following the basic formula below.

BASIC SMOOTHIES

Makes 2 smoothies

Special Equipment:
High-powered blender

1½ cups water or nut milk (page 70)

Squeeze of citrus (lemon, orange, lime, or grapefruit)

1 cup fruit

2 cups vegetable

Small handful of herbs (optional)

1 tablespoon healthy fats, coconut oil, nuts, or seeds (optional)

2 pinches of extras (such as grated ginger, turmeric, spices, powders) (optional)

Add all of the ingredients to the blender and blend on high until smooth. Add a couple ice cubes, if you like, and blend again until smooth. Serve immediately, or you can store in an airtight container (mason jars work well) for 1 to 2 days in the fridge.

White // Oatmeal + Tahini + Date

1½ cups nut milk

1 cup cooked oatmeal, or 1 cup oats soaked in nut milk overnight

Drizzle of tahini

2 dates, pitted

Dash or two of cinnamon

White ingredients:

- Cauliflower
- Rolled oats
- Cooked quinoa
- Sesame seeds
- Hemp seeds
- Tahini
- Ginger
- Cashews
- Coconut oil
- Banana

Red // Strawberry + Goji Berry + Basil + Ginger + Cinnamon

1½ cups water or nut milk

1 cup strawberries

2 tablespoons goji berries

1 thumbnail-size piece of ginger, peeled

2 basil leaves

Dash or two of cinnamon

Red Ingredients:

- Red pepper
- Beets
- Cranberries
- Pomegranate
- Gogi berries
- Raspberries
- Strawberries
- Cherries
- Watermelon
- Apple
- Cayenne

Orange // Carrot + Orange + Turmeric

1½ cups water or nut milk

1 carrot

1 ripe banana

Pulp of 1 orange

1 thumbnail-size piece ginger, peeled and chopped

1 teaspoon coconut oil

½ teaspoon turmeric

Orange Ingredients:

- Carrot
- Squash
- Sweet potato
- Turmeric
- Mango
- Apricot
- Orange

Yellow // Pineapple + Coconut Milk + Bee Pollen

1 cup canned full-fat coconut milk

½ cup water

½ cup diced pineapple

1 ripe banana

1 yellow pepper

1 teaspoon bee pollen + more for sprinkling on top

1 thumbnail-size piece of ginger, peeled (optional)

Yellow Ingredients:

- Yellow pepper
- Yellow carrots
- Yellow beets
- Turmeric
- Lemon
- Bee pollen
- Banana
- Pineapple

Green // Spinach + Avocado + Mint + Spirulina

1½ cup water or nut milk

Handful of spinach or kale

½ avocado

1 ripe banana

1 tablespoon coconut oil or manna

3 to 4 mint leaves

1 tablespoon spirulina (optional)

Green Ingredients:

- Spinach
- Kale
- Swiss Chard
- Dandelion greens
- Celery
- Cucumber
- Mint
- Parsley
- Cilantro
- Basil
- Avocado
- Green Apple
- Kiwi
- Spirulina

Blue/Purple // Blueberries + Chia + Banana

2 cups water or cashew milk

1 cup blueberries

1 ripe banana

1-inch piece of ginger, peeled and sliced

1 tablespoon chia seeds

Blue / Purple Ingredients:

- Purple cabbage
- Blueberries
- Blackberries
- Acai

Blk // Cacao + Almond Milk + Almond Butter

1½ cups almond milk or other nut milk

1 tablespoon cacao powder

2 dates, pitted

1 tablespoon almond butter

1 tablespoon black sesame seeds (optional)

1 tablespoon chia seeds (optional)

1 to 2 teaspoons maca (optional)

Brown / Black Ingredients:

- Black Sesame Seeds
- Chia Seeds
- Nut or Seed Butter
- Cacao
- Raisins
- Dates

BLUEBERRY BOTTOM BUCKWHEAT
WITH TAHINI + MAPLE + CASHEW MILK

1 cup frozen wild or regular blueberries

2 cups cashew milk + more for serving (page 70)

1 cup water

¼ teaspoon sea salt

1 cup whole buckwheat

1 tablespoon maple syrup

2 teaspoons tahini

¼ teaspoon cinnamon

This is another super-simple way to switch up the porridge routine, when you are looking for a grain other than oats, and for something on the semi-sweeter side. Whole buckwheat can usually be found with oatmeal and breakfast cereals, but you should also be able to find it in the bulk food section of the grocer. If you don't have buckwheat on hand, you can make this with oats or quinoa, following their specific cooking times. This is a great make-ahead breakfast, and usually I store any extra in jars in the fridge so I have breakfast ready to go a couple days out of the week. If you're making this ahead of time, add the splash of milk right before serving.

Take the blueberries out of the freezer and allow them to thaw as you prepare everything else.

Put 2 cups of the cashew milk, the water, and salt in a medium saucepan and bring to a boil. Stir in the buckwheat, reduce the heat to low, cover, and cook for 10 minutes. Uncover, turn the heat off, and stir in the maple syrup, tahini, and cinnamon.

Divide the blueberries among 4 bowls or jars. Add the buckwheat on top, leaving some room for the milk. If you're enjoying right away, add a splash of the cashew milk on top. You can also keep this in an airtight jar in the fridge for a few days, and add the milk when you're ready to enjoy.

MISO OATS WITH SCALLIONS
+ SESAME OIL

1 tablespoon ghee or
neutral oil

1 cup quick-cooking
rolled oats

1 teaspoon red miso

3 cups + 1 tablespoon water

2 scallions, white and light
green parts only, minced

Drizzle of toasted sesame oil

2 pinches of sesame seeds
or Nori Gomasio (page 31)

Handful of microgreens or
sprouts (optional)

I often rely on oatmeal for a quick breakfast, and adding miso and scallions is a simple way to switch up my routine when I am in the mood for savory, umami flavors in the morning. You could also add other toppings such as walnuts, chopped spinach, or even a poached egg.

———————

Heat the ghee in a medium saucepan over medium-low heat. Add the oats, and toast for about 2 minutes, until lightly browned. In a small bowl, dilute the miso with 1 tablespoon of the water. Stir the miso in with the oats, then add the 3 cups water (be careful, it may splatter) and stir. Bring to a simmer, reduce the heat to low, and cook for about 5 minutes, stirring occasionally, until it has reduced to a desired porridge/oatmeal consistency. Remove from the heat and divide between 2 bowls. Add the scallions, sesame oil, sesame seeds, and microgreens or sprouts, if using, or any other topping you like.

BANANA + OAT + CARDAMOM PANCAKES

2 ripe bananas

1 cup rolled oats

¼ to ½ cup almond or cashew milk (page 70)

Pinch of sea salt

Pinch of cardamom

Pinch of cinnamon

2 to 4 tablespoons ghee, coconut oil, or olive oil

Drizzle of maple syrup or honey (optional)

Handful of berries or sliced banana (optional)

I have always been skeptical of the one- or two-ingredient pancake recipes that are floating around on the Internet. Pancakes were a special weekend breakfast treat for me as a kid, so messing with the original is something I am open to only if it tastes the same or even better. The first time I made this three-ish ingredient pancake, all that changed, and after having one of these flavorful, fluffy hotcakes, I have never looked back to a flour-heavy pancake again. One of the best things about these is that you can make the batter a day or two in advance, so they are that much easier to whip up in the morning.

_____

Put the bananas, oats, milk, salt, cardamom, and cinnamon into a food processor and blend until smooth. The amount of milk you need varies greatly on how ripe the bananas are, so start with ¼ cup and add more, a tablespoon at a time, until the mixture runs smooth and is pourable.

Heat 2 tablespoons of ghee or oil in a large cast iron pan over medium heat. Pour ¼ cup of the batter onto the pan. I cook no more than two at a time so as not to overcrowd the pan. Cook, undisturbed, for 2 to 3 minutes, until the pancake is golden brown on one side, then flip and cook for 2 to 3 more minutes, until golden brown on the second side. Transfer to a plate and continue until you have no more batter, adding another tablespoon or so of ghee or oil between batches as needed. Serve immediately, warm, with maple syrup and fruit, if using, or any other toppings you choose.

SWEET POTATO + CHICKPEA + POBLANO HASH WITH A FRIED EGG

2 sweet potatoes, peeled

1 large onion

1 large poblano pepper, deseeded

One 14-ounce can chickpeas, drained and coarsely chopped

1 teaspoon sweet paprika

½ teaspoon kosher salt

Freshly ground black pepper

1 tablespoon ghee or neutral high-heat oil

2 to 4 eggs

Extra virgin olive oil

While I have a serious love for traditional hash made with white potatoes, this hash breaks that tradition with the addition of chopped chickpeas, and the swap from white to the more nutrient-dense sweet potatoes. It also gets a kick of spice thanks to the poblano. It's a great weekend breakfast that can easily feed a crowd. The fried egg is optional, but it makes this more of a main meal instead of a breakfast side dish.

———————

Using a cheese grater, grate the sweet potato into a large bowl, along with the onion, then the poblano. Add the chopped chickpeas, paprika, salt, and pepper to taste, and stir to combine. Take a paper towel, and press it firmly on top of the sweet potato mixture to release as much of the moisture as you can.

Heat the ghee in a cast iron pan over medium-high heat. Add the sweet potato mixture and spread it out evenly in the pan. Let it cook, undisturbed, for 5 minutes, or until crispy on the bottom. Using a spatula, flip the mixture (in pieces is fine) and cook on the other side for 8 to 10 minutes, until browned and crispy.

Either while the hash is cooking or when the hash is done, fry the eggs. Heat the olive oil in a large frying pan over medium-low heat, and crack in no more than 2 eggs (away from each other). Cover the pan and cook for 3 to 5 minutes, until the eggs are cooked to your liking. I prefer the whites to be cooked through but the yolks a little runny—covering the pan helps achieve that perfect balance. When the eggs are done cooking, place them on top of the hash and serve.

CHICKPEA CREPES (THREE WAYS)

Chickpea crepes are a delicious, savory vehicle for ingredients like smashed avocado, hummus, a fresh tomato-cucumber salad, or soft scrambled eggs. I make these for breakfast often because they are easy to whip up when you want something filling and crepe-like. I usually double or triple the batter, and keep any extras in a container in the fridge for when I crave them (which is often) and can easily fry up a couple, or for when I want to feed a bunch of friends for brunch. In addition to relying on the classic batter, I also love to play around and add spices, herbs, and other items to give the batter a little boost of flavor. The basic recipe is great for just about everything, especially smashed avocados with just a squeeze of lime. Adding cumin and jalapeño to the batter gives it a nice, spicy, aromatic kick and is best paired with a simple tomato-cucumber salad. The crepes are also perfect topped with scrambled eggs, along with some paprika and scallions. These are just some suggestions, so feel free to experiment with different toppings and additions to the basic recipe. The batter keeps for several days in the fridge.

Basic Chickpea Crepe + Smashed Avocado

Makes about 4 crepes

1 cup chickpea flour

1 cup water

3 tablespoons extra virgin olive oil

½ teaspoon kosher salt

Ghee or extra virgin olive oil, for cooking

1 avocado, roughly smashed (optional)

Squeeze of lime (optional)

Put the chickpea flour, water, olive oil, and salt in a medium mixing bowl and whisk until combined. Allow the batter to sit, at room temperature, for about 30 minutes. Alternatively, you can store this batter in an airtight container in the fridge for up to 1 week.

Heat a large cast iron or frying pan over high heat. When the pan is hot, lower it to medium heat and add enough ghee or olive oil to coat the bottom of the pan. Add about ½ cup of the batter, using a ladle, and spread the batter (just slightly) using the back of the ladle. The pancake should be slightly thinner and larger in circumference than a more traditional pancake, about ⅛ inch thick. Cook for 2 to 3 minutes on each side. The crepe is ready to flip when you see some bubbles popping on the surface. Transfer to a plate and top with the smashed avocado and lime, if using, or any toppings of your choice.

Cumin + Jalapeño Crepe with Tomato + Cucumber Salad

Makes about 4 crepes

1 batch Basic Chickpea Crepe recipe

1 teaspoon cumin

1 jalapeño, deseeded and minced

Handful of cilantro, roughly chopped

Tomato + Cucumber Salad

1 dozen cherry tomatoes, halved

1 cucumber, chopped

1 avocado, chopped

Handful of arugula, chopped

Drizzle of extra virgin olive oil

Squeeze of lemon or lime juice

Sea salt

Freshly ground black pepper

Prepare the Basic Chickpea Crepe batter, and stir in the cumin, jalapeño, and cilantro. Follow cooking instructions for the Basic Chickpea Crepe.

Tomato + Cucumber Salad

In a large bowl, toss the tomatoes, cucumber, avocado, and arugula together, add the olive oil and lemon juice, and season with salt and pepper. Serve the salad on top of the cooked chickpea crepe.

Paprika Chili Crepe + Soft Scrambled Eggs with Chives

Makes about 4 crepes

1 batch Basic Chickpea Crepe recipe

1 teaspoon paprika

½ teaspoon chili powder

1 scallion, white and light green parts only, minced

2 tablespoons minced chives

Sea salt

Freshly ground black pepper

4 eggs, lightly beaten

2 tablespoons extra-virgin olive oil

Prepare the Basic Chickpea Crepe batter, and stir in the paprika, chili powder, and scallion. Follow cooking instructions for the Basic Chickpea Crepe.

Stir the chives, and a pinch of salt and pepper into the beaten eggs. Heat the oil in a medium pan over medium-low heat. Add the egg mixture and cook while continually stirring (the secret to a soft scramble is to always be stirring). The eggs take a little longer to cook (about 7 minutes), but they come out soft and creamy. Serve on top of the cooked crepes.

CAULIFLOWER "GRITS" WITH CRISPY SHIITAKES + SPINACH

3½ ounces (8 to 10) shiitakes, thinly sliced

2 tablespoons sunflower oil (or other neutral oil)

1 tablespoon tamari or coconut aminos

1 tablespoon extra virgin olive oil

2 handfuls of spinach

Sea salt

Freshly ground black pepper

Squeeze of lemon juice

1 head cauliflower, cut into florets (about 4 cups)

3 tablespoons ghee or extra virgin olive oil

1 tablespoon fresh thyme, minced

1 tablespoon chickpea flour

1 cup Vegetable Broth (page 108) or Simple Bone Broth (page 111) or water

Splash of (unsweetened) milk of your choice (optional)

My husband and I got engaged in New Orleans, which is also where he went to college. So we have a special connection to that city, its culture, and its food. Whenever we go, we always find the amount of butter and lard used in the cooking kind of amusing since it's not used as liberally where we live in the Northeast, and it is certainly different from how we cook at home. Michael loves to order the classic shrimp and grits when we visit—a great example of that butter and cream indulgence. This version is a healthier spin with the use of cauliflower, ghee, and broth, still a delicious, satisfying breakfast, perfect for a lazy Sunday morning.

———————

Preheat the oven to 350°F. Put the shiitakes on a small baking sheet, and toss them with the sunflower oil and tamari. Roast for 15 to 20 minutes, until crispy around the edges. Set aside.

Heat the olive oil in a large pan or wok over medium heat, add the spinach, and cook for about 2 minutes, until lightly wilted. Season with salt and pepper and a squeeze of lemon juice. Remove from the pan, and set aside until you're ready to assemble.

Use the same pan to cook the grits. But first, put the cauliflower florets in a food processor and pulse until it resembles a fine grain. Do not run the food processor continuously and be careful not to overprocess, or else it will turn to mush. Heat 2 tablespoons of the ghee in the pan over medium heat and add the cauliflower. Sauté for about 2 minutes, until tender, then add the thyme and a pinch of salt and pepper and give it a good stir. In a small bowl whisk the flour in the broth or water to dissolve, then add it to the cauliflower and cook for about 5 minutes, until it reduces by about two-thirds. Divide the cauliflower among a couple of bowls, splash some milk on top, if using, and top with the spinach and shiitakes.

MILKS

If you were to peek inside my refrigerator, you would quickly learn that I am a big fan of homemade nut milk. After I made milk for the first time, I never wanted it from a box again—it is so smooth and creamy that there really is no comparison, and if you have a high-powered blender, it is a breeze to make. What was once intimidating has now become a weekly ritual. I use my milks in smoothies, coffee, tea, or just for enjoying on their own.

I like to interchange my nut and seed milks, and which type I make is often dictated by what I have on hand. If I want something quick, I will use a nut or seed that does not need straining or much soaking. If I have more time and prepare ahead (usually on the weekends), I will usually make almond milk or another nut milk that requires an overnight soak and a strain. This chart makes it easy for you to figure out how to make a nut or seed milk using what you have on hand.

GENERAL METHOD FOR MAKING MILKS

makes 4 cups

3 cups of water to 1 cup of nuts or seeds for regular milk

makes 3 cups

2 to 1 for cream (thicker consistency)

makes 2 cups

1 to 1 for yogurts, sauces

Milk add-ins

- Pinch of sea salt
- 1 teaspoon vanilla extract
- 1 tablespoon coconut oil
- Optional sweeteners: pitted dates, maple syrup, honey

Add the nuts and the desired amount of water to the blender and blend on high for about 2 minutes, until super-smooth and creamy. Add in any additions, such as sea salt or coconut oil, and sweetener, if using, and blend again until incorporated. Strain the nut milk through a nut milk bag or cheesecloth, if necessary (see chart). Transfer to a jar and store in the fridge when not in use. Depending on the type of nuts and their freshness, this will last for 2 to 5 days in the fridge.

Nuts / Seeds	Soak Time (hrs)	Straining
Almonds	8–12	✓
Brazil nuts	8–12	✓
Cashews	0–3	—
Hemp	—	—
Hazelnuts	8–12	✓
Macadamia Nuts	3	—
Oats	—	—
Pistachios	3	—
Sesame seeds	—	—
Sunflower seeds	—	—
Walnuts	8–12	✓

Strawberry Almond Milk

2 cups almond milk

½ cup strawberries

Dash of cinnamon

1 tablespoon coconut oil

Golden Milk

1 cup cashew or hemp milk

1 teaspoon turmeric

2 teaspoons honey

Pinch of cinnamon

Pinch of cardamom

Pinch of nutmeg

2 teaspoons coconut oil

Chocolate Chia Milk

2 cups walnut or Brazil nut milk

1 tablespoon cacao

1 tablespoon chia seeds (optional)

1 teaspoon maple syrup

1 teaspoon vanilla extract

Green Milk

2 cups pistachio milk

1 teaspoon spirulina

1 teaspoon honey

CARAWAY TOMATO BAKED EGGS

3 tablespoons extra virgin olive oil

1 large yellow onion, sliced

1 large red pepper, sliced

1 large clove garlic, minced

1 teaspoon ground caraway

1 teaspoon paprika

½ teaspoon cumin

Pinch of cayenne (optional)

½ teaspoon kosher salt

One 28-ounce can pureed tomatoes

4 to 6 eggs

Handful of chopped cilantro or parsley (optional)

2 scallions, white and light green parts only, minced (optional)

Toasted almonds for serving (optional)

While there are many variations of baked eggs out there, this version has the aromatic rye flavor of caraway that complements both tomatoes and eggs so well. Cooking the eggs on the stovetop and covering the pan is a more foolproof way to get those perfectly runny yolks, since you can lift the lid and easily check on them every few minutes until they are done and to avoid overcooking the eggs.

———————

Heat the oil in a large frying pan over medium heat. Add the onion and red pepper and cook, while stirring, for about 5 to 7 minutes, until they are soft and starting to brown. Add the garlic, and cook for another 2 minutes. Add the caraway, paprika, cumin, cayenne, if using, and salt, and stir until the vegetables are evenly coated. Add the tomatoes, and stir to combine. Simmer for about 5 minutes, then lower the heat just slightly to medium-low. Using a spoon, make a well in the mixture and carefully break an egg into the well. Do this for each egg that you are using, distributing them evenly throughout the pan. Once all of the eggs have been nestled into the tomato mixture, cover the pan, and cook for 8 to 10 minutes, until the whites are set but the yolks are still a little runny. Finish with cilantro, scallions, or nuts, if using, or any toppings you like, and serve immediately.

HOMEMADE PUFFED RICE CEREAL

1 cup short-grain brown rice

1¾ cups water

Sea salt

2 cups sunflower oil (or other neutral high-heat oil)

Did you grow up eating Rice Krispies? I loved them so much as a kid, but now I am not a big fan of cereal that comes from a box. When I learned that I could easily make crispy rice cereal at home, I became obsessed. It takes a few steps, but they are easy steps. Feel free to make a double or triple batch like I do, so that it lasts you awhile. I serve this with a splash of homemade chocolate or vanilla nut milk (see page 70). As a little bonus, you can also use puffed, crispy rice as a topper for so many things. It adds a lovely crunch to soups, salads, or even desserts.

—————

Put the rice, water, and pinch or two of salt into a medium saucepan. Bring to a boil, cover, and reduce to a simmer. Cook for 40 minutes. Remove from the heat and let it sit, covered, for another 10 minutes.

Preheat the oven to 250°F. Spread the rice out onto a small baking sheet. Bake (dehydrate) in the oven for 2 hours. The rice should be dry and hard when it's done. Put the rice in the fridge to cool off for at least 1 hour.

The last step is the most important: puffing the rice. Line a large plate with paper towels. In a medium saucepan, add enough oil so that it comes up about ½ inch on the sides (you may need more or less than the 2 cups), and heat the oil over medium heat until it's shimmering. Test to make sure it's ready by adding a single piece of rice to the oil. If it sizzles all around the rice kernel, then it's ready. Add about half of the rice to the saucepan and cook for about 30 seconds, just until the rice puffs up. This happens very quickly, and you do not want to overcook it, otherwise the rice will be too crunchy. Use a slotted spoon to remove the rice and place it on the paper towel–lined plate. Do this until all of the rice is puffed. It will keep for a couple of weeks in an airtight (preferably glass) container on the counter.

SOUP

There is no simpler way to nourish yourself than with a bowl of soup. No matter what time of year, soup is always there—as a warm hug in the winter or as a cool refresher in the summer. When I make a soup I want it to be easy to prepare but sophisticated, with layers and layers of flavor. To do this I like to use different spices and acidity to brighten up and add complexity to the soup with very little effort. I also love to add toppings and texture to my soups, making it feel even more interesting, satisfying, and like a full meal. One of the best things about making soup is that it can be frozen and reheated easily, so I would recommend making a big or double batch if you want to have something quick and healthy to eat waiting for you in the freezer.

SOUPS

Minestrone with Quinoa and Arugula + Walnut Pesto   80

Broccoli + Tahini Soup with Broccoli Stem Ribbons   83

White Bean Soup with Cumin Seed + Lemon + Crispy Sprout Leaves   84

Cucumber Avocado Gazpacho with Nori Gomasio   87

Roasted Zucchini Soup with Coriander Seed + Coconut Milk + Crispy Squash Blossoms   88

Sun Gold Tomato Gazpacho with Toasted Almonds + Chives   91

Roasted Delicata Squash + Greens + Turmeric Broth   92

Ginger Miso Butternut Squash Soup with Roasted Apples   94

Cauliflower Hazelnut Soup with Fried Sage   96

Curried Sweet Potato + Yellow Split Pea Stew with Crispy Shallots   99

Creamy Mushroom Miso Soup with Gomasio + Toasted Sesame Oil + Scallions   100

French Lentil + Squash Stew with Caraway + Crispy Kale   103

Parsnip Chowder with Garlic Chips   104

Ginger + Garlic + Cilantro Congee   107

Broth (Four Ways)

   Vegetable Broth   108

   Mushroom Broth   110

   Lemongrass Broth   110

   Simple Bone Broth   111

MINESTRONE WITH QUINOA AND ARUGULA + WALNUT PESTO

4 tablespoons extra virgin olive oil

1 small fennel bulb, white and green parts only, diced

1 medium white onion, diced (about 2 cups)

1 white potato, peeled and diced (about 1 cup)

1 tablespoon sea salt

1 teaspoon dried thyme

Red pepper flakes

4 or 5 cloves garlic, thinly sliced

One 14-ounce can white cannellini beans, drained and rinsed

6 cups water

3 handfuls of leafy greens (kale, spinach, Swiss chard, bok choy, depending on what's in season)

1 cup cooked quinoa

2 tablespoons Arugula + Walnut Pesto (page 24)

This soup is a celebration of green veggies no matter the season. In the dead of winter, it celebrates dark leafy greens; when spring comes around, it highlights those bright, vibrant greens that start to make their way to the markets again. I love this soup for its versatility but also for that arugula pesto swirling around on top, giving it some extra zing. If you're planning to make this ahead of time, I recommend adding the greens right before serving to keep them from losing their vibrant hue.

———————

Heat the oil in a large, heavy-bottomed pot over medium heat, and add the fennel and onion. Cook for several minutes, until they have softened. Add the potato, salt, thyme, and red pepper flakes to taste, stir, and cook for about 5 minutes, until the potato has softened slightly. Add the garlic and cook for another 2 minutes, while stirring. Add the beans and water, bring to a boil over medium heat, then reduce to a simmer. Simmer for about 1 hour.

Add the greens, and stir until they wilt. This should take only 2 to 5 minutes. Add the quinoa and stir. Remove the soup from the heat. Ladle the soup into individual serving bowls and add a spoonful (or more, if you like) of the pesto on top. The soup will keep for several days in an airtight container in the fridge.

BROCCOLI + TAHINI SOUP WITH BROCCOLI STEM RIBBONS

Special Equipment:
Immersion blender

¼ cup extra virgin olive oil
+ more for drizzling

1 large onion, diced (about 2 cups)

1 clove garlic, minced

1 head broccoli, cut into florets, stem
reserved for roasting

2 teaspoons sea salt + more
for seasoning

Freshly ground black pepper

4 cups water

¼ cup tahini + more for drizzling

2 pinches Nori Gomasio (page 31)
or sesame seeds (optional)

Drizzle of toasted sesame oil
(optional)

Tahini might seem like an unexpected ingredient for soup, but if you've never tried it you will be surprised at how its nutty flavor really enhances this particular soup. We all know that tahini loves vegetables, and when it's blended with broccoli and onions, it makes everything in this soup come alive. You can also get creative with toppings here; however, I'd strongly suggest some sesame seeds and a drizzle of sesame oil in addition to the broccoli stems, since they go hand in hand with the tahini.

——————

Preheat the oven to 400°F.

Heat the oil in a heavy-bottomed pot over medium heat. Add the onion and cook for several minutes, until the onion is very soft. Add the garlic and cook for 2 more minutes. Add the broccoli and salt and pepper and cook for several minutes, stirring often, until tender. Add the water, bring to a boil, reduce to a simmer, and cook for 30 minutes.

Meanwhile, peel the outer layer (⅛ inch) of the broccoli stem, then peel lengthwise to create ribbonlike pieces. Line a large baking sheet with parchment. Place the broccoli stem pieces on it, drizzle with olive oil, and season with salt and pepper. Bake for about 20 minutes, until tender and golden brown around the edges.

Use an immersion blender or transfer the soup to a blender, and blend until smooth. Add the tahini, and blend until combined. Divide the soup among 4 bowls, and add the broccoli stem ribbons, gomasio and sesame oil, if using, and any additional toppings you like. Serve warm. This soup will keep for a few days in an airtight container in the fridge.

WHITE BEAN SOUP WITH CUMIN SEED + LEMON + CRISPY SPROUT LEAVES

Special Equipment:
Immersion blender; mortar and pestle

¼ cup extra-virgin olive oil + more for drizzling

1 large yellow onion, sliced

½ teaspoon cumin seeds, coarsely ground

3 cloves garlic, minced

½ to 1 teaspoon kosher salt

Freshly ground black pepper

One 14-ounce can white beans, drained

5 cups water

10 to 15 Brussels sprouts, leaves separated

Juice of 1 lemon (about 2 tablespoons)

I think it is good to have a combination of both dried and canned beans on hand in the pantry. Dried beans pack more flavor and nutrients, but canned beans are great when you want to make something quick, like this soup. When shopping for canned beans, I always look for brands that are organic and stored in cans that have a BPA-free lining.

I love soups with just a few ingredients—one bright spice that really stands out, a splash of acidity, a topping for texture contrast. This soup has all of those elements and is also very forgiving and versatile. Substitute any beans that you have in your pantry if you don't happen to have white beans on hand.

———

Heat the olive oil in a medium, heavy-bottomed pot over medium heat. Add the onion and cumin seeds, and cook until the onion is soft and starting to brown. Add the garlic, salt, and pepper to taste and cook for another 2 minutes while stirring. Add the white beans and water, bring to a boil, reduce to a simmer, and cook for about 30 minutes.

Preheat the oven to 350°F. Spread out the Brussels sprout leaves evenly on a baking sheet, drizzle with olive oil, add half of the lemon juice, season with salt and pepper, and give them a gentle toss to coat. Roast until they are crispy and the edges are starting to brown, 8 to 10 minutes.

Add the remaining lemon juice to the soup, and using either an immersion blender or a stand blender, blend the soup until silky smooth. Taste and adjust any seasoning you think is necessary. Ladle the soup into bowls, top with a handful of the crispy sprout leaves, and serve warm. This soup will keep for a few days in an airtight container in the fridge.

CUCUMBER AVOCADO GAZPACHO
WITH NORI GOMASIO

¼ cup extra virgin olive oil

½ cup water

2 tablespoons white wine vinegar

½ teaspoon sea salt

Pinch of red pepper flakes

½ avocado

2 large cucumbers, chopped

1 tablespoon diced shallots

1 small clove garlic, minced

1 tablespoon Nori Gomasio (page 31) or sesame seeds (optional)

Drizzle of toasted sesame oil (optional)

This is such a refreshing chilled soup for a warm summer day. All you need to do is add the ingredients to a blender, and in two minutes it's ready to sip on. The avocado creates a nice creamy texture, and the nori gomasio is the perfect, simple, salty, crunchy condiment to sprinkle on top. If you do not have gomasio handy, use plain sesame seeds instead.

————————

Put the olive oil, water, vinegar, salt, red pepper flakes, avocado, cucumbers, shallots, and garlic into a blender and blend until smooth. Taste and adjust any other seasoning that you feel necessary. Chill in the fridge for a minimum of 1 hour before serving. Divide among 4 bowls, and top each with gomasio and sesame oil, if using. This is best if enjoyed immediately, but will keep for a day or two in an airtight container in the fridge.

ROASTED ZUCCHINI SOUP WITH CORIANDER SEED + COCONUT MILK + CRISPY SQUASH BLOSSOMS

Special Equipment:
Mortar and pestle

1 large yellow onion, chopped into ½-inch pieces

3 medium zucchini, chopped into ½-inch pieces

3 cloves garlic, minced

1 teaspoon coriander seeds, coarsely ground

1 teaspoon kosher salt

Freshly ground black pepper

3 tablespoons extra virgin olive oil + 2 tablespoons for the zucchini blossoms

4 zucchini blossoms, pestle removed (optional)

2 cups water

Juice of ½ lemon (about 1 tablespoon)

4 tablespoons canned full-fat coconut milk

I'll let you in on a little secret: the simple marriage of roasted zucchini and coriander seed results in enormous flavor. That's why this is one of my favorite soups in the book. Zucchini, when roasted and caramelized, has a beautiful depth that complements coriander's bright finish. This soup has the kind of complexity you would expect from a much more labor-intensive soup but with very little effort.

———————

Preheat the oven to 400°F.

Put the onion, zucchini, and garlic on a baking sheet, and toss with the coriander, salt, pepper to taste, and the 3 tablespoons of olive oil. Bake for 30 minutes, or until the veggies are soft and starting to brown around the edges.

While the veggies are roasting, sauté the zucchini blossoms, if using. Heat the 2 tablespoons of oil in a small frying pan over medium heat. Add the zucchini blossoms and cook for about 3 minutes on each side, until wilted and crisp. Remove and set aside until you're ready to serve the soup.

Transfer the roasted zucchini mixture to a blender, and add the water and lemon juice. Blend on high until silky smooth. Divide the soup among 4 bowls, and finish each with a tablespoon of the coconut milk and a zucchini blossom, if using. This soup will keep for a couple of days in an airtight container in the fridge.

SUN GOLD TOMATO GAZPACHO WITH TOASTED ALMONDS + CHIVES

½ cup (chilled) Vegetable Broth (page 108) or Lemongrass Broth (page 110)

½ teaspoon kosher salt

1 small clove garlic

1 teaspoon white wine vinegar

2 tablespoons extra virgin olive oil

1 pint yellow Sun Gold tomatoes or any small variety

1 cucumber, peeled and chopped

½ cup slivered almonds

1 tablespoon sunflower oil

Handful of chives, minced

Last summer I cooked for a friend's charity event and was asked to make an appetizer. It was the middle of July, one of the hottest months of our summer, so the first thing I thought to make was a chilled gazpacho. That was how this yellow tomato gazpacho came to be, and I knew I had to share the recipe someday because so many people asked me for it that night. While I love using yellow tomatoes because they are so pretty and extra sweet, any smaller variety of tomato, such as red grape tomatoes, will do. Also, if you want to make this quickly and you don't have broth on hand, feel free to use water and adjust the seasoning to taste

———————

Put the broth, salt, garlic, vinegar, olive oil, tomatoes, and cucumber in a blender, and blend until smooth. Set aside, or keep covered in the fridge until ready to serve. This soup gets better with time, and is even better served a day later. It will keep for a few days in a airtight container in the fridge.

When you're ready to serve, toast the almonds. Heat the sunflower oil in a frying pan over medium-low heat and add the almonds. Cook for a couple of minutes, undisturbed, until golden brown. Stir, and cook for a couple more minutes, then remove the almonds from the pan. Distribute the soup among bowls, and top with the toasted almonds and a sprinkle of the chives.

ROASTED DELICATA SQUASH + GREENS + TURMERIC BROTH

1 Delicata squash, deseeded and sliced into half moons

Drizzle of extra virgin olive oil

Sea salt

Freshly ground black pepper

1 tablespoon coconut oil

1 yellow onion, thinly sliced

4 or 5 cloves garlic, smashed and coarsely chopped

1-inch piece fresh turmeric, peeled and grated, or 2 teaspoons ground turmeric

2 tablespoons chickpea miso or mellow white miso

4 cups water + 3 tablespoons for the miso

Juice of 1 lemon (about 2 tablespoons)

2 handfuls of leafy greens (kale and bok choy; Swiss chard, escarole, and dandelion greens also work well)

Pea shoots for serving (optional)

Cooked brown rice or quinoa for serving (optional)

During the colder months, and particularly in the middle of winter, I like to eat an abundance of warming turmeric root and dark, leafy greens to keep my immune system in check. This soup is one of the best ways to get a big serving of both of these immune builders. It comes together in a flash and takes very little prep work, so I make it when I am busy but need that extra boost of nourishment and anti-inflammatories.

———————

Preheat the oven to 400°F. Place the squash onto a baking sheet, drizzle with olive oil, and season with salt and pepper. Cook for 30 to 40 minutes, until the squash is soft and brown around the edges.

Melt the coconut oil in a medium pot over medium heat. Add the onion and cook for 5 to 7 minutes, until it is soft and starting to brown. Add the garlic and turmeric and cook for 2 more minutes, while stirring. In a small bowl, dissolve the miso in 3 tablespoons of water. Add the miso/water mixture and the rest of the water to the pot, bring to a boil, reduce to a simmer, and cook for 30 to 40 minutes. Add the lemon juice and the leafy greens, stir, and cook for about 2 minutes, until they are soft.

Ladle a few large spoonfuls of the broth into 2 bowls, and finish with the roasted squash and pea shoots and rice, if using, or any additional toppings. This is best if enjoyed immediately, but it will keep for a day or two in an airtight container in the fridge.

GINGER MISO BUTTERNUT SQUASH SOUP WITH ROASTED APPLES

Special Equipment:
Immersion blender

1 medium butternut squash (about 3 pounds), cut in half and deseeded

Drizzle of extra virgin olive oil

Sea salt

Freshly ground black pepper

3 tablespoons ghee or extra virgin olive oil

1 medium yellow onion, diced (about 2 cups)

1 teaspoon minced ginger

3 cloves garlic, minced

2 tablespoons apple cider vinegar

¼ cup chickpea miso or mellow white miso

3 cups water + 1 cup for the miso

Red pepper flakes (optional)

1 apple, cored and thinly sliced

2 tablespoons grapeseed oil

This is a wonderful soup to celebrate the arrival of fall, when squash starts to appear at the farmers' markets, and the apples are perfect for picking. If you don't have butternut squash, any kind of squash with a hard skin would work. The umami kick from the miso and the crunchy sweetness of the apples create a sophisticated harmony of flavors for such a simple soup. You can serve this with or without the apples, but I love the additional pop of texture and flavor they give.

———

Preheat the oven to 400°F. Place the butternut squash on a baking sheet, drizzle with olive oil, and season with salt and pepper. Roast the squash for 30 to 35 minutes, until tender. Remove and cool until you're able to handle the squash. Using a spoon, scoop the flesh from the skin and discard the skin, or save it to make vegetable broth.

Heat the ghee in a large, heavy-bottomed pot over medium heat. Add the onion and cook for about 10 minutes, until soft and just starting to brown. Add the ginger and garlic and cook for about 2 minutes, just enough to release their flavor. Add the apple cider vinegar, and deglaze by cooking for a minute or two until the vinegar has evaporated, while scraping any bits that are sticking to the bottom of the pan. Add the squash, and stir to coat it with the ginger-onion mixture. In a small bowl, dissolve the miso in 1 cup of water. Add the miso broth and the remaining water to the pot. Give it a good stir, add the red pepper flakes (if using), and allow the mixture to simmer over medium-low heat (do not bring to a boil). Cook for 10 to 15 minutes to allow the flavors to develop.

While the soup is simmering, roast the apples. Lower the oven temperature to 375°F. Place the apples on a baking sheet in one layer, so they are all touching the pan, and drizzle with the grapeseed oil. Bake for 15 to 20 minutes, until the apples are browned and crisp. Be sure to keep a close eye on them, because they can quickly turn from brown to burnt. Set aside until you're ready to serve.

Puree the soup. Puree only half if you want to leave a little texture, or puree it all if you prefer a smooth soup. Use an immersion blender or pour the desired amount into a blender, and blend until you have the texture you desire. Add it back to the remaining soup in the pot and stir. Ladle the soup into individual bowls, add the fried apples on top, and serve. This will keep for a few days in an airtight container in the fridge.

CAULIFLOWER HAZELNUT SOUP
WITH FRIED SAGE

½ cup hazelnuts + 1 to
2 tablespoons for topping (optional)

¼ cup extra virgin olive oil

1 small leek, white and light green
parts only, chopped

One 2½- to 3-pound cauliflower
head, roughly chopped

2 teaspoons sea salt

Freshly ground black pepper

2 cloves garlic, minced

8 cups Vegetable Broth (page 108)

Juice of ½ to 1 lemon (about
1 to 2 tablespoons) or white
wine vinegar

1 to 2 tablespoons sunflower oil
(or other high-heat oil)

6 to 8 sage leaves

Roasted cauliflower pieces for
serving (optional)

Chives or scallions for serving
(optional)

Cauliflower, hazelnuts, and sage are the ultimate comfort flavors when the crisp weather hits. This is one of my go-to soups—especially when I am cooking for larger parties or for friends and family at home. As with most soups, this only gets better after sitting and allowing the flavors to develop, so if I am serving this for a party, I usually make it a day or two before, always making sure that I save a little extra for myself.

———————

Preheat the oven to 350°F. Put the hazelnuts on a baking sheet and bake for 15 to 20 minutes, until the skins start to peel away and they are a lightly browned. Be careful not to burn them because the flavor of the nuts will change dramatically. When they are done, allow them to cool slightly, then roll the nuts between your hands or a paper towel to release the skins. Discard the skins and set the peeled hazelnuts aside while you prepare the soup.

Heat the olive oil in a heavy-bottomed pot over medium heat. Add the leeks and sauté for a couple of minutes, until they are soft. Add the cauliflower, salt, and pepper. Cook for about 10 minutes, stirring occasionally, until the cauliflower starts to brown, being careful not to burn the leeks. Add the garlic and cook for another 2 minutes.

Add in the vegetable broth and bring to a boil, reduce to a simmer, place a cover loosely over the top, and cook for 20 to 30 minutes. Carefully transfer the soup to a blender. Add in ½ cup of the toasted hazelnuts and 1 tablespoon of the lemon juice. Blend until you have a smooth puree. Taste and adjust any seasoning as necessary. You might want to add a little more salt and maybe another tablespoon of lemon juice. Keep the soup in the blender while you prepare the sage.

In a small cast iron frying pan, heat the sunflower oil over medium heat. Fry the sage leaves for about 2 minutes on each side, until they become nice and crispy. Remove and place on a paper towel.

Pour the warm soup into individual bowls. Chop the extra hazelnuts and use them for topping, along with some black pepper, cauliflower or chives, if using, and any other toppings you like.

This soup is best served warm, right away. It also makes great leftovers and will keep for several days in an airtight container in the fridge.

CURRIED SWEET POTATO + YELLOW SPLIT PEA STEW WITH CRISPY SHALLOTS

3 cups peeled and diced sweet potatoes (about 3 potatoes)

2 tablespoons extra virgin olive oil

3 tablespoons ghee or extra virgin olive oil

1 medium yellow onion, diced (about 2 cups)

3 large cloves garlic, minced

2 teaspoons curry powder

Freshly ground black pepper

1 cup yellow split peas (dal), rinsed

5 cups water

1 tablespoon sea salt

Juice of ½ lemon (about 1 tablespoon)

Coconut milk for serving (optional)

Crispy Shallots for serving (optional; page 30)

This is one of those soups that I came up with by looking in my pantry for inspiration. I always seem to have yellow split peas on hand, but I wasn't sure what to do with them until I made this vibrant and comforting stew. Now I make sure my yellow split peas are stocked to make this soup, and several different variations of it. I think of this as a forgiving pantry meal—even if you do not have sweet potatoes in your kitchen, you can throw this soup together without them, or you can use squash or carrots. As always, the toppings, in this case the Crispy Shallots, are optional but highly recommended.

———————

Preheat the oven to 400°F. Put the sweet potatoes on a baking sheet, toss with the olive oil, and bake for 20 minutes, or until soft. Roughly mash the potatoes with a fork and set aside.

Heat the ghee in a heavy-bottomed pot over medium heat. Add the onion and cook for about 5 minutes, until the onion is soft. Add the garlic, curry powder, and pepper and cook for another 2 minutes (do not add salt at this point). Then add the split peas, mashed sweet potato, and the water. Gently stir the mixture and bring it to a boil. Reduce to a simmer, partially cover, and cook for 30 to 40 minutes, until the split peas are soft. Add the salt and lemon juice, and stir. Simmer for an additional 10 minutes. Keep on low heat until you're ready to serve. Pour the soup into 4 bowls, finish with a drizzle of coconut milk, and top with Crispy Shallots, if using. This soup will keep for several days in an airtight container in the fridge. Be sure to store the crispy shallots separately in an airtight container on the counter. They will keep for a couple of days.

CREAMY MUSHROOM MISO SOUP WITH
GOMASIO + TOASTED SESAME OIL + SCALLIONS

Special Equipment:
Immersion blender

2 tablespoons ghee

3 cloves garlic

7 scallions, sliced, white
and green parts separated

5 cups shiitake mushrooms, sliced +
2 additional caps, sliced, for serving
(optional)

Two 6-inch pieces kombu

5 cups water

3 tablespoons red miso

Pinch of Nori Gomasio (page 31)

Drizzle of toasted sesame oil

Sunflower oil for frying (optional)

This dream team of mushrooms, miso, and sesame seeds is so comforting in the fall and wintertime. Miso and mushrooms both have medicinal properties, and this soup is just as nourishing as it is flavorful. This is the kind of soup you could serve to someone who needs a little extra love, but it would also be a wonderful starter at a dinner party.

———————

Heat the ghee in a heavy-bottomed pot over medium heat. Add the garlic and the white parts of the scallion, and cook for about 2 minutes, until soft. Then add the 5 cups of mushrooms, and cook until soft, about 3 minutes.

Add the kombu and water, and allow to simmer for 30 minutes. Remove the kombu and discard, add the miso, and cook for another 10 minutes, or longer, to allow the flavors to develop. Use an immersion blender or transfer to a blender and puree.

Divide among a few bowls, and garnish with the green parts of the scallion, gomasio, and a drizzle of sesame oil. If using, sauté the remaining mushrooms in sunflower oil until crisp, and top each bowl of soup with a few.

FRENCH LENTIL + SQUASH STEW WITH CARAWAY + CRISPY KALE

1 large acorn squash, deseeded and cut into wedges

3 tablespoons extra virgin olive oil or ghee + drizzle for the squash and kale

Sea salt

Freshly ground black pepper

1 medium onion, diced (about 2 cups)

3 carrots, diced (about 1 cup)

3 cloves garlic, minced

One 14½-ounce can organic diced tomatoes

1 teaspoon ground caraway

1½ cups French green lentils, rinsed

6 cups Vegetable Broth (page 108) or water

1 large bunch of kale, destemmed and roughly chopped (about 3 cups)

Lentil soup was one of my mom's staples when I was growing up. I requested it often, and it was one of the first recipes I asked her for when I started cooking for myself. While I have altered her original recipe very little, I now like to add squash to the soup as well as caraway seed, which gives it a welcome hint of rye flavor. If you don't have or are not into caraway, feel free to leave it out. One more thing—if you don't want your soup topped with crispy kale, you can also coarsely chop it and add it directly to the soup or leave it out altogether.

———————

Preheat the oven to 425°F. Line a baking sheet with parchment paper and put the squash on it, drizzle with olive oil, and season with salt and pepper. Bake for 30 to 40 minutes, until soft and the edges are starting to brown. Once the squash is cool enough
to handle, remove the skin and cut the squash into cubes.

Heat the 3 tablespoons of oil in a large heavy-bottomed pot over medium heat, add the onions and carrots, and cook for 8 to 10 minutes, until they become very soft. Add the garlic, and cook for another 2 minutes. Add the tomatoes along with their juices, then add the caraway. Cook for about 2 minutes to reduce the tomato juices. Add the lentils and the cubed squash, stir, and add the broth. Bring to a boil, reduce to a simmer, cover partially, and cook for 35 to 40 minutes. Taste the soup and add more salt, if necessary.

Put the kale on a baking sheet, drizzle with olive oil, and season with salt and pepper. Cook for 15 to 20 minutes, until crisp.

To serve, ladle the soup into individual bowls, and top with a handful of the crispy kale. This soup will keep for several days in an airtight container in the fridge.

PARSNIP CHOWDER WITH GARLIC CHIPS

Special Equipment:
Immersion blender

4 tablespoons ghee or extra virgin olive oil

1 large yellow onion, diced (about 2 cups)

4 cups peeled and diced parsnips

4 cups peeled and diced potatoes

½ teaspoon dried sage

1 teaspoon kosher salt

Freshly ground black pepper

2 cloves garlic, thinly sliced

4 cups Vegetable Broth (page 108)

2 cups unsweetened cashew milk (page 70)

2 tablespoons Garlic Chips (page 30)

When I was a kid growing up in New England, clam chowder was of course one of my favorites, especially when we went on vacation to visit family in Cape Cod. This recipe is a nod to an old-fashioned clam chowder, minus the dairy and minus the clam. Instead, it has parsnips swimming around with the potatoes to give it a grown-up, modern, delicious root vegetable twist.

———————

Heat the ghee in a large, heavy-bottomed pot over medium heat. Add the onion, and cook for about 5 minutes, until soft. Add the parsnips and potatoes, and cook for 10 to 12 minutes, stirring frequently, until the vegetables are tender. Add the sage, salt, pepper, and garlic, and cook, while stirring, for another 2 to 3 minutes. Then add the broth and cashew milk, bring to a simmer, and cook for 30 to 40 minutes. Using an immersion blender or a stand blender, blend only a quarter to half of the soup, leaving some texture and chunks. Distribute among individual bowls and serve warm with a pinch of Garlic Chips on top of each. This will keep for a few days in an airtight container in the fridge.

GINGER + GARLIC + CILANTRO CONGEE

1-inch piece ginger, peeled and thinly sliced

3 cloves garlic, thinly sliced

1 cup long grain white rice

6 cups Vegetable Broth (page 108) or Simple Bone Broth (page 111) or water

Handful of chopped cilantro

Pinch of Nori Gomasio (page 31) or sesame seeds (optional)

Microgreens or minced scallions for serving (optional)

Tamari or coconut aminos for serving (optional)

If I had to choose the most comforting, feel-good soup in this book, it would have to be this congee. I was introduced to congee on a trip to China, where they serve it for breakfast, and it was such a warming, delicious way to start the day. Congee is simply rice that has been cooked for a long time with lots of extra water until it breaks down and becomes smooth and creamy. I make congee often, for breakfast or lunch, when the weather calls for it, or when I am craving something simple and comforting. The ginger and garlic make it extra warming and flavorful. This would also be great served with a poached egg on top or with the Olive Oil Poached Fish (page 200).

Put the ginger, garlic, rice, and broth in a large stockpot over high heat, bring to a boil, and reduce to a simmer. Cook for about 1 hour, stirring occasionally so the rice does not clump together. When the congee is thick and creamy, it is ready to serve. Ladle into individual bowls, and top with some chopped cilantro. If using, add gomasio, microgreens, tamari, or any other additional toppings. This is best served immediately, but it will keep for several days in the fridge. To reheat, you will want to add a splash of water to the congee.

BROTH (FOUR WAYS)

Broths are the foundation of flavorful cooking and are an important tool in my kitchen. I like to keep my broths well-stocked—I feel more secure when I have homemade broth in my fridge or freezer. Making broth is often a weekend project for me, especially in the winter, when I use broth almost every other day to make soup or cook up a grain or lentil. A few broths, such as lemongrass, are staples in my summer recipes. Another great reason to keep broth around is for sipping, either alone or with a handful of spinach or some grated turmeric or ginger for a little immunity boost. The following are a few broth recipes that I like to rotate making, some of which are interchangeable in certain recipes and some that have very specific uses.

Vegetable Broth
Makes about 10 cups of broth

2 tablespoons extra virgin olive oil

2 large yellow onions, peeled and cut down the center

1 large carrot, cut in half down the center and then into 4 pieces

1 tablespoon tomato paste

1 head garlic, halved down the center

1 tablespoon black peppercorns

1 tablespoon sea salt

5 sprigs thyme

1 bay leaf

10 cups water

This is the mother of my broth family. It is the most versatile, and I use it in many of my soups and other recipes. If you have never tried adding tomato paste to broth, I encourage you to try it in this version. It adds a richness and umami to the broth, and it is also a great way to use up the tomato paste that tends to sit in the back of the fridge once it's opened. For certain recipes, when you might want a clearer broth, you can omit the tomato paste.

Heat the oil in a large, heavy-bottomed pot over medium heat. Add the onions and carrot, cut side down, and cook for about 5 minutes, until black and charred. Add the tomato paste and toast it for 1 or 2 minutes. Add the garlic, peppercorns, salt, thyme, and bay leaf and enough water to fill the pot—about 10 cups—leaving 1 or 2 inches of room from the top of the pot. Bring to a boil, then reduce the heat to low to create a slow and lazy simmer. Simmer for 1 to 2 hours, taste, and when it has the desired flavor, remove the broth from the heat and allow it to cool for about 30 minutes. Strain, and either use immediately or transfer to glass jars. Allow it to cool for about 1 hour before placing in the fridge or freezer. This broth will keep in the fridge for about 1 week, or in the freezer for up to 6 months.

Mushroom Broth

Makes 8 cups of broth

1 large onion

3 cloves garlic, peeled

3 cups dried shiitake mushrooms

2 sprigs thyme

8 cups water

2 large pieces kombu
(about 2 ounces)

Mushroom broth is a great substitute for a heavier beef broth. It has a wonderful umami punch and is great for cooking grains or rice or for making risotto. I also enjoy it as a sipping broth in the winter (much like the Shiitake Mushroom Tea on page 152).

Put the onion, garlic, mushrooms, and thyme in a heavy-bottomed pot and add the water. Bring to a boil, reduce to a slow simmer, and cook for 2 hours.

Remove the broth from the heat, add the kombu, and allow it to sit for about 30 minutes. Strain the broth and use right away, or transfer to glass container to store for later use. This broth will keep in the fridge for up to 1 week or in the freezer for up to 6 months.

Lemongrass Broth

Makes 5 to 6 cups of broth

6 cups water

3 stalks fresh or dried lemongrass

One 2-inch piece ginger,
peeled and sliced

6 cloves garlic

1 medium onion, sliced into
thick chunks

1 tablespoon sea salt

1 tablespoon black peppercorns

I think of this lovely, aromatic broth as more of a summertime broth. It has a subtle lemongrass flavor and could be served simply over some noodles or rice and veggies. This broth is best used as a base for light and refreshing summertime soups—you'll find it in the Sun Gold Tomato Gazpacho (page 91).

Put all of the ingredients in a heavy-bottomed pot, bring to a simmer, and cook at a low, lazy simmer for 1 to 2 hours. Strain the broth, and either use right away or transfer to a large glass jar and reserve for later. This will keep for about 1 week in the fridge or about 6 months in the freezer.

Simple Bone Broth
Makes about 12 cups of broth

1½ pounds bones from organic, grass-feds cows

16 cups (1 gallon) water

2 teaspoons apple cider vinegar

1 tablespoon sea salt

1 tablespoon black peppercorns (optional)

Fresh herbs such as rosemary or thyme (optional)

Spices such as fennel or cumin seeds (optional)

Fresh veggies such as onions, carrots, or celery (optional)

Bone broth is one of the simplest, most delicious, and powerful ways you can nourish yourself, especially in the colder months when winter and cold season are in full force. Bone broth is known to be great for the gut, and when our guts are happy, we are happy. Besides being super-nutritious, it is also easy and inexpensive to make. Depending on your butcher, they might give away the bones for free, but don't skimp on quality for free bones. Bones from organic, grass-fed cows are strongly recommended because you want to make sure you're getting the very best nutrients. All it takes to make bone broth is a few basic ingredients, and about twelve hours of very low simmering. The apple cider vinegar is in there to coax out the nutrients. Feel free to add other herbs or spices to flavor the broth; however, I often use only the bones, vinegar, and salt because the broth is so flavorful it does not need much else. I often use this broth as a base for soups that call for any kind of broth (even vegetable) for its simple but rich flavor.

Put the bones, water, vinegar, salt, and, if using, any other adds-ins, such as black pepper, herbs, spices, and veggies, into a large heavy-bottomed pot. Cover with a tight-fitting lid and simmer on very low heat for 12 hours. Check on it every few hours, and add more water if needed; you want to make sure the bones are always covered with the water.

Strain the broth, and either use right away or transfer to a couple of glass jars and reserve for later. If you are keeping it in the fridge, you will notice that a layer of fat forms on the top once it has solidified. When you go to use your broth, simply skim the fat off the top and reserve it for cooking, or you can discard. You will also notice that the broth turns to a gelatinous consistency once it's chilled. This is good! You want that consistency, because it's packed with nutrients, however, don't worry if your broth is more liquid than gelatinous. You will still be getting a lot of good benefits. If you are freezing the broth, it's best to do this in wide-mouth glass containers, and make sure to leave about an inch of free space toward the top to allow for the liquid to expand. This will keep for about 1 week in the fridge or about 6 months in the freezer.

SALADS

Salad is a lunchtime ritual for me, but I hardly ever
think of salad as just some dressed greens in a bowl.
Salads are a great vehicle for a variety of grains, a
colorful array of vegetables, and even a few legumes, nuts,
and seeds. They are a wonderful way to get creative and
experiment with different flavor combinations and also as a
way to purge the fridge of any extra veggies, herbs, or cooked
grains that might be hanging around. I like my salads to be on
the filling side when serving them for lunch, but if they are a
side dish, I prefer them much simpler and lighter. This chapter
is a collection of some of my favorite everyday salads—with a
few special-occasion salads thrown in for good measure. Salad
recipes, in my mind, are often more of an inspiration guide
with lots of flexibility, so take that inspiration and run with it
depending on what you have on hand, what's in season, what
your body is craving, or what your senses are telling you.

SALADS

Wild Rice Salad with Snap Peas +
Avocado + Radish + Sesame Ginger
Dressing   117

Honey Roasted Nectarines + Kale with
Dukkah, Pine Nut, and Oat Croutons   118

Snap Pea + Broccoli Stem Slaw with Basil
Cilantro Aioli   121

Rainbow Garden Salad with Eggplant +
Cherry Tomatoes + Zucchini + Arugula +
Quinoa   122

Cucumber Noodle Pad Thai   125

Roasted Summer Veggies + Scallion Miso
Butter   126

Warm Corn Salad with Chives + Sesame
Seeds + Smoked Paprika   127

Roasted Eggplant Salad with Rice
Noodles + Green Herb Tahini   128

Everyday Farmers' Market Greens +
Grains Salad   131

Crispy Green Bean Salad with Toasted
Almonds and Everyday Shallot +
Mustard Vinaigrette   132

Grilled Kale Caesar with Pickled
Onions   135

Charred Cauliflower + Fennel Salad
with Quinoa + Arugula + Raisins   136

Deviled Brussels Sprout Salad   139

Shaved Brussels Sprout + Fennel Salad
with Mandarins + Avocado + Ginger
Mustard Vinaigrette   140

WILD RICE SALAD WITH
SNAP PEAS + AVOCADO + RADISH
+ SESAME GINGER DRESSING

Special Equipment:
Microplane

½ cup wild rice

1 cup water

1 clove garlic

1-inch piece ginger

3 tablespoons brown rice vinegar

3 tablespoons sunflower oil

2 tablespoons toasted sesame oil

1 teaspoon coconut aminos
or tamari/soy sauce

1 avocado, sliced

1 cup snap peas, sliced on the bias

1 watermelon radish, thinly
sliced into half moons

I like to add rice to my salad—it gives it great texture and makes a salad feel like a full meal. I am even more inclined to throw in some rice when I have leftovers from the night before. While I prefer this salad with wild rice for its firm texture and nutty taste, it can also be made with any kind of rice you have on hand—white, brown, or even black could be used instead.

———————

Cook the rice. Add the rice and water to a small saucepan. Bring to a boil, cover, reduce to a simmer, and cook for 45 minutes. Remove from the heat and allow to sit for 10 minutes. Transfer the rice to a large bowl.

While the rice is cooking, make the dressing. Grate the garlic and ginger into a small mixing bowl using a Microplane. Add the vinegar, oils, and coconut aminos to the bowl and whisk to combine.

Pour half of the dressing over the rice, and stir. Add about half of the avocado, peas, and radish, and a drizzle more of the dressing, and toss to combine. Finish with the remaining veggies on top and another drizzle of the dressing.

HONEY ROASTED NECTARINES + KALE WITH DUKKAH, PINE NUT, AND OAT CROUTONS

Dukkah Croutons

1 cup quick-cooking rolled oats

¼ cup oat flour

½ cup pine nuts or sunflower seeds

3 tablespoons extra virgin olive oil

1 large egg white

3 tablespoons Pumpkin
Seed Dukkah (page 29)

Sea salt

Roasted Nectarines

5 nectarines, pitted and sliced

1 tablespoon sunflower oil

1 tablespoon honey

To Serve

Bunch of kale, deribbed,
or mesclun greens

Drizzle of extra virgin olive oil

1 teaspoon Champagne vinegar

¼ teaspoon sea salt

I never used to like fruit in my salad. And now, not only do I like it, but I have an appreciation for how the sweetness can balance out the other savory elements in the salad. The sweet caramelized nectarines in this luscious salad are the perfect complement to the savory dukkah croutons. The croutons can be made in advance, and they are a delightful topping for almost any salad.

————————

Dukkah Croutons
Preheat the oven to 300°F. Put all the ingredients for the croutons in a large bowl, and stir to combine. Line a baking sheet with parchment and spread the mixture out evenly on it. Bake for 30 to 40 minutes, until lightly browned on top. Allow to cool before breaking the dukkah into clusters. You can do this days in advance: the croutons will keep for about 1 week in an airtight container on the countertop.

Roasted Nectarines
Turn up the oven to 350°F. Line another baking sheet with parchment and place the sliced nectarines on it. Drizzle with the sunflower oil and honey, toss to coat, and arrange them so they are evenly dispersed. Bake for 30 minutes, or until the nectarines are browned and caramelized around the edges.

To Serve
While the nectarines are roasting, dress the kale with the olive oil, vinegar, and salt, and rub it into the kale until it wilts and breaks down. Set aside until you're ready to serve.

Divide the kale among a couple of serving bowls. Place the nectarines on top, and carefully break off pieces of the dukkah and serve them on top.

SNAP PEA + BROCCOLI STEM SLAW
WITH BASIL CILANTRO AIOLI

1 cup snap peas, thinly sliced lengthwise

1 cup broccoli stems, outer ⅛ inch peeled and cut into matchsticks (about 2 stems)

1 cup shredded green cabbage

1 cup shredded purple cabbage

Basil Cilantro Aioli

1 large handful cilantro, finely chopped

6 basil leaves, finely chopped

1 clove garlic, minced

Juice of ½ lemon (about 1 tablespoon)

⅓ cup mayonnaise

Sea salt

Freshly ground black pepper

Years ago, I was inspired to throw some snap peas into a slaw, and now I never make slaw without them. I am also a big fan of incorporating broccoli stems into salads because they are fresh and crunchy, just like the snap peas. Both the broccoli stems and the snap peas are exactly what a good crunchy slaw is begging for. This slaw is great to make when you have leftover broccoli stems in the fridge (so be sure you don't throw them away!)—however, if you don't happen to have them around, just add some extra cabbage. Same goes if snap peas are not in season—feel free to leave them out and add more cabbage and/or broccoli stems.

———————

Put the snap peas, broccoli stems, and cabbages in a large bowl and toss to combine.

Basil Cilantro Aioli

In a small bowl, whisk together the cilantro, basil, garlic, lemon juice, and mayonnaise, and season with salt and pepper.

To Serve

Pour the aioli over the snap peas, stems, and cabbage, and toss until everything is combined. You can make this a day or so ahead and keep covered in the fridge until you're ready to serve.

RAINBOW GARDEN SALAD WITH EGGPLANT + CHERRY TOMATOES + ZUCCHINI + ARUGULA + QUINOA

Roasted Vegetables

2 large Japanese eggplants
(the long, thin variety), cubed

2 medium zucchinis, cubed

1 pint cherry tomatoes,
sliced in half

Drizzle of extra virgin olive oil

Sea salt

Freshly ground black pepper

Quinoa

1 cup quinoa, rinsed

2 cups water

Sea salt

3 tablespoons extra
virgin olive oil

1 tablespoon Champagne
or white wine vinegar

Freshly ground black pepper

To Serve

2 large handfuls of arugula

If you come to my house in the summer, chances are that I will serve you this easy-to-throw-together salad. It is a weekly standby in the summer when my garden, the farm stand, and the supermarkets are overflowing with eggplant, tomatoes, and zucchini. Simply roasted with some olive oil, all in the same pan, the flavors represent the best of the summer season.

———————

Roasted Vegetables

Preheat the oven to 400°F. Line a large baking sheet with parchment paper and put the veggies on it (I like to keep the veggies separate, but it's fine to mix them all together if you prefer). Drizzle the olive oil over the veggies and season with salt and pepper.

Roast for 30 to 40 minutes, until all of the veggies are tender and caramelized.

Quinoa

Put the quinoa and water in a medium saucepan with a pinch of salt. Bring to a boil, cover, reduce to a simmer, and cook for 15 minutes. Once the quinoa is done cooking, remove the lid, fluff with a fork, and allow to cool. I like the quinoa to be at room temperature for this salad, so I spread it out onto a small baking sheet and put it in the fridge until I am ready to serve, however, this is optional. Feel free to serve it warm if you prefer. When the quinoa is cooled to your liking, toss it with the olive oil and vinegar, and season with salt and pepper.

To Serve

In a large serving bowl, first add the arugula, then the quinoa, and finish with the veggies on top. I like to arrange the veggies each in a row, to look like a rainbow.

CUCUMBER NOODLE PAD THAI

Special Equipment:
Spiralizer or julienne peeler

2 cucumbers, julienned or spiralized lengthwise

1 medium zucchini, julienned or spiralized lengthwise

1 medium yellow zucchini, julienned or spiralized lengthwise

Up to ¼ cup Sweet + Spicy Peanut Sauce (page 37)

3 scallions, white and light green parts only, thinly sliced

¼ cup peanuts or cashews, finely chopped

Handful of cilantro, roughly chopped

7 to 10 basil leaves, roughly chopped

Nori Gomasio (page 31) for serving (optional)

Toasted sesame or hemp seeds for serving (optional)

When the weather gets warm, I love making light salads with raw veggie noodles. I especially love using delicious sauces and preparations from dishes that would typically use a regular pasta or noodle, just like this "pad Thai" recipe. To make the noodles, you can use a spiralizer or the more humble (but just as effective) julienne peeler. If you have neither, I would recommend starting with the julienne peeler. It's an inexpensive investment that will end up getting a lot of use.

———————

In a large bowl, toss together the cucumber and zucchini noodles. Spoon in the peanut sauce little by little until the veggie noodles are dressed as much as you like. Toss to make sure all of the noodles are evenly coated. Sprinkle the scallions, nuts, cilantro, and basil, and the gomasio and seeds, if using, or any other toppings that you like, and serve immediately.

Spiralizing cucumbers can be a bit tricky, and you usually end up with a little less yield than you do from zucchini, which is why I included two cucumbers in the recipe. Be sure to chop up and save any cucumber that doesn't get spiralized for another use or just add them on top of this salad.

ROASTED SUMMER VEGGIES + SCALLION MISO BUTTER

2 Japanese eggplants (the long, thin variety), sliced lengthwise

2 medium zucchinis, sliced lengthwise

2 tablespoons + drizzle of sunflower oil (or other neutral oil)

1 pint cherry tomatoes, halved

2 tablespoons Scallion Miso Butter, at room temperature (page 27)

Here are some other roasted or sautéed veggies and fruit that would be great with miso butter:

- Squash + Red onion
- Artichoke hearts + Fava beans
- Snap Peas + Okra
- Leeks + Sweet potato
- Crispy fingerling potatoes + Scallions
- Apples + Yellow onion

Once you've tried miso butter, it is hard to not want to cover everything in it all the time. There is something about that salty, umami miso flavor mixed with the richness of butter that is so irresistible. While I cannot think of a single vegetable that would not be better with miso butter, grilled summer vegetables such as eggplant and tomatoes tend to be an extra-yummy pair. With that said, feel free to toss any vegetable that is in season with miso butter. You will not be disappointed.

Preheat the oven to 400°F. Place the eggplant and zucchini on a large baking sheet, and brush both sides with the oil. Add the tomatoes to the baking sheet and drizzle with oil. Roast for 30 to 40 minutes, until the veggies are tender, browned, and caramelized.

Transfer the roasted veggies to a large serving bowl, toss with the miso butter, and serve warm.

WARM CORN SALAD WITH CHIVES + SESAME SEEDS + SMOKED PAPRIKA

2 tablespoons ghee or extra virgin olive oil

4 ears corn, kernels removed

Sea salt

Freshly ground black pepper

¼ teaspoon smoked paprika

¼ cup minced chives

3 tablespoons white sesame seeds

2 tablespoons mayonnaise (optional)

I spend my summers in a place where dozens of farm stands claim to have the best corn around. Mid- to late summer, when the corn is plentiful and in its prime, it becomes a dinnertime staple in our house. Sometimes it's simply grilled in the husk, and sometimes I shave the kernels from the corn and add them to a salad. This super-simple salad is my preferred way to highlight tasty summer corn. While the corn is the main event here, the sesame seeds add another layer of crunch and texture, and the smoked paprika does what it does best by adding a punch of smoky flavor.

———————

Heat the ghee in a cast iron or frying pan over medium heat. Add the corn kernels and cook for 3 to 5 minutes, until tender, and season with salt and pepper.

Transfer the corn to a serving bowl, and toss with the smoked paprika, chives, sesame seeds, and mayonnaise, if using, and serve.

ROASTED EGGPLANT SALAD WITH RICE NOODLES + GREEN HERB TAHINI

1 medium eggplant, cut into large cubes (about 3 cups)

3 to 4 tablespoons extra virgin olive oil

Sea salt

Freshly ground black pepper

8 ounces soba or rice noodles

¼ cup Green Herb Tahini (page 38)

Nori Gomasio (page 31) for serving (optional)

Scallions or microgreens for serving (optional)

I make green tahini often, so when I had some extra lying around one day I decided that combining it with roasted eggplant would be the perfect way to use it up. I added the dressing to some rice noodles, and with one twirl and bite of the noodle, tahini, and eggplant combination, it became one of my favorite salads of all time. Rice noodles always feel like such a treat, but when you coat them with this herbaceous, tangy tahini, all of the ingredients really come alive.

———————

Preheat the oven to 400°F.

Place the eggplant on a large baking sheet, and generously drizzle with olive oil. Eggplant is very absorbent, so you want to make sure you use enough oil to evenly coat all of the pieces. Season with salt and pepper, and roast for 30 minutes, or until tender and golden brown.

While the eggplant is cooking, cook the noodles according to the instructions on the package. Strain, transfer to a bowl, and toss with about half of the tahini.

When the eggplant is finished cooking, add it to the bowl, drizzle a little more tahini over the top, and toss to combine. Add the gomasio or greens, if using, or any additional toppings and serve.

EVERYDAY FARMERS' MARKET GREENS + GRAINS SALAD

2 very large handfuls of greens in season (spinach, arugula, kale, romaine)

1 cup cooked grain: quinoa, millet, farro

1½ cups beans: white, black, kidney

⅓ cup nut or seed: pine nuts, hazelnuts, cashews, almonds, sesame seeds, sunflower seeds, pumpkin seeds

⅓ to ½ cup Everyday Shallot + Mustard Vinaigrette (page 39) or Lemon Caper Vinaigrette (page 40)

Here are some other ideas for delicious additions to this quick and easy salad:

- Avocado + Chilled leftover roasted salmon

- Sautéed onion + Sweet potato

- Pears + Walnuts

- Macadamia Ricotta (page 158) + Figs

- Shiitake mushrooms + Asparagus

This is the basic formula I use for both my everyday lunchtime salad and a more simple salad that I prepare as a side dish. The greens are always inspired by what I find at the market, and I often mix and match varieties as well as the other add-ins suggested. If I am making this for myself for lunch, I might include a grain, a bean, a nut, and some sliced avocado, but if I am serving it as a brunch side dish I might include only the greens and a nut, lightly tossed in a dressing.

Put the salad greens, grains, beans, and nuts or seeds that you are using into a large serving bowl. Spoon a couple tablespoons of the dressing over the top and toss to combine. Continue to dress the salad until it is to your liking. Add any additional veggies or other additions on top, if you're using, spoon a little more dressing over the veggies, and serve.

CRISPY GREEN BEAN SALAD WITH TOASTED ALMONDS AND EVERYDAY SHALLOT + MUSTARD VINAIGRETTE

3 tablespoons sunflower oil

½ cup slivered almonds

1 pound green beans, trimmed

⅓ cup Everyday Shallot + Mustard Vinaigrette (page 39)

Nori Gomasio (page 31) for serving (optional)

Microgreens for serving (optional)

I like my green beans charred and crispy, with a little bit of bite left to them. This simple salad gets finished with some toasted almonds for extra crunch and my classic shallot vinaigrette. This is the perfect salad to serve at a summer lunch or dinner but would also be great on a holiday table in the winter.

———————

Heat 1 tablespoon of the oil in a cast iron pan over low heat. Add the almonds, and cook for a couple of minutes, stirring only once or twice, until golden brown. Remove from the pan. Add 2 more tablespoons of oil to the same pan, raise the heat to medium, and add the green beans. Cook for several minutes, stirring every once in a while, until the beans are crispy and starting to char on the outside. Transfer to a serving platter, toss with the vinaigrette, and finish with the almonds and a sprinkle of gomasio and handful of microgreens, if using.

GRILLED KALE CAESAR
WITH PICKLED ONIONS

Bunch of kale (about 10 to 12 leaves), deribbed

Drizzle of sunflower oil (or other neutral high-heat oil)

⅓ cup Classic or Vegan Caesar Dressing (pages 40 to 41)

1 small red onion, quick pickled (page 27)

Grilling greens, tossing them in dressing, and serving them as a salad is a great party trick. Cooking the greens brings out so much flavor with such little effort. The pickled onions add a lively contrast flavor to break up the overall richness of a Caesar dressing. Of course, if it is not grill weather, you can do this on a super-hot grill pan or a cast iron skillet and get the same effect. Also, feel free to use either the Classic or the Vegan Caesar Dressing—both are equally delicious here.

———————

Heat the grill or grill pan to medium-high heat. Toss the kale with the oil and lightly massage it into the leaves. Put the kale on the grill or grill pan and cook for about 2 minutes on each side, until it starts to crisp on the edges. Transfer to a serving platter, and allow to cool slightly for a couple of minutes. Drizzle with the dressing, top with the pickled onions, and serve.

CHARRED CAULIFLOWER + FENNEL SALAD
WITH QUINOA + ARUGULA + RAISINS

½ cup quinoa, rinsed

1 cup water

Sea salt

4 tablespoons grapeseed oil
(or other neutral oil)

1 small yellow onion, sliced

1 small fennel bulb, sliced

2 cloves garlic, minced

½ cup raisins or currants

2 tablespoons red wine vinegar

1 small head cauliflower, cut
into florets, with one flat side

Freshly ground black pepper

2 handfuls of arugula

The flavor of fennel has a mellow sweetness when it's cooked, and the combination of caramelized fennel and cauliflower is irresistible. This simple technique of charring the cauliflower in a cast iron pan or skillet is a wonderful way to bring out those deep flavors that I love so much. The sweetness of the raisins pairs perfectly with the richness of the caramelized vegetables, making this a supremely delicious, warm, fall or winter salad.

———————

Put the quinoa, water, and pinch of salt in a medium saucepan, bring to a boil, reduce to a simmer, cover, and cook for 15 minutes. When the quinoa is done, transfer it to a serving bowl to cool.

Heat 2 tablespoons of the oil in a cast iron pan or skillet over medium heat. Sauté the onion and fennel for 8 to 10 minutes, until soft and starting to brown. Add the garlic and raisins and cook for another 2 minutes. Transfer the cooked onion mixture to the quinoa, add the red wine vinegar, and toss to combine all the ingredients.

In the same pan, heat the remaining 2 tablespoons of oil over medium-high heat. When the pan is very hot, add the cauliflower, flat sides touching the pan, and season lightly with salt and pepper. This is important, to get a nice char on one side of the floret. Let them cook, undisturbed, for 4 to 5 minutes, until they are charred on one side. Give them a stir, and cook for another 2 minutes, or until the cauliflower is tender. Add it to the bowl with the quinoa.

Add the arugula to the bowl with the quinoa and cauliflower, gently toss to combine, and serve immediately.

DEVILED BRUSSELS SPROUT SALAD

3 hard-boiled eggs

2 tablespoons mayonnaise

1 teaspoon Dijon mustard

2 teaspoons hot sauce

¼ teaspoon kosher salt

5 scallions, white and light green parts only, thinly sliced

4 cups Brussels sprouts (about 30), sliced in half

2 tablespoons sunflower oil (or other neutral high-heat oil)

Sea salt

Freshly ground black pepper

I wasn't quite sure what to call this salad. It is pretty much a hybrid of a deviled egg and a crispy Brussels sprout salad. Taking a hard-boiled egg and mixing it up with the same kind of ingredients in a spicy deviled egg filling makes for an incredibly rich and extremely tasty sauce to coat those crispy sprouts. So, if you like both deviled eggs and crispy Brussels sprouts as much as I do, then you're going to love this salad.

—————

Mash up the hard-boiled eggs with the mayonnaise, mustard, hot sauce, salt, and scallions, and keep in the fridge until you're ready to serve.

Cook the sprouts. Heat the oil in a large cast iron pan over medium-high heat. Add the sprouts to the pan, flat sides down. Cook undisturbed for about 5 minutes, until the sprouts are charred on that one side. Give them a stir and continue to cook for another 2 to 4 minutes, until the sprouts are fork-tender. Season lightly with salt and pepper. Transfer them to a serving bowl and allow them to cool slightly.

Pour the egg sauce over the sprouts, toss to combine, and serve warm.

SHAVED BRUSSELS SPROUT + FENNEL SALAD WITH MANDARINS + AVOCADO + GINGER MUSTARD VINAIGRETTE

Special Equipment:
Mandoline

10 Brussels sprouts, thinly sliced

1 small fennel bulb, white parts only, thinly shaved with a mandoline

½ cup Spicy Ginger Sesame Mustard (page 38)

1 mandarin or other kind of orange, segmented

1 avocado, thinly sliced

¼ cup pistachios, finely chopped

Citrus season brings bright, vibrant colors to the kitchen in the dead of winter. This salad has those fresh flavors that will make you forget the cold outside. It's also easy to throw together and would make a great fancy side dish salad for a dinner party. Because oranges, avocado, and fennel can usually be found year-round, you can make this salad anytime, subbing any green or cabbage you like for the sprouts.

———————

Put the sliced sprouts and shaved fennel in a medium mixing bowl, pour the Spicy Ginger Sesame Mustard over the top, and toss to coat. To serve, divide the sprouts and fennel among 4 individual plates, place the mandarin slices and avocado on top, and finish with the chopped pistachios.

NIBBLES + SNACKS

Because I like to eat many small meals and snacks throughout the day, I am always looking for simple, fun ways to keep myself fueled. I don't have a huge sweet tooth, so you will find that all of my nibbles are on the savory side and most of them involve vegetables. I also believe that keeping things around such as homemade hummus or sheets of nori or rice paper for wrapping up leftovers makes snacking healthier. And when healthy homemade nibbles are more accessible to you, you are less likely to reach for the processed, packaged snack food.

NIBBLES + SNACKS

CRISPY CURRIED SWEET POTATO CHIPS

Special Equipment:
Mandoline

2 sweet potatoes,
2 to 3 inches in diameter

2 tablespoons extra virgin olive oil

1 tablespoon curry powder

½ teaspoon garlic powder

Pinch or two of cinnamon

Maldon sea salt to finish

The key to getting crisp oven-baked sweet potato chips is to hold the salt until they are done cooking. The salt draws the moisture out of the potato and makes for a soggy chip. These chips are great for snacking, and even better as a crunchy topping for soups or salads.

———

Preheat the oven to 325°F.

Using a mandoline, slice the sweet potatoes into ⅛-inch-thick rounds (about 3 cups). Put the sliced sweet potatoes in a large mixing bowl, and toss with the olive oil, curry powder, garlic powder, and cinnamon until evenly coated.

Lay out the sliced potatoes on a large baking sheet, making sure no pieces are overlapping or they will not crisp properly. You will likely need to do two batches, but do not cook two sheets at the same time because each needs to be in the center of the oven to cook evenly.

Bake the chips for about 15 minutes. Pull them out of the oven, flip each chip using tongs, and then return the sheet to the oven for another 15 minutes. Keep an eye on them and take out any that start to brown on the edges. When they are done, transfer the chips to a wire rack to cool. Don't be alarmed if they are not super-crisp yet. They will harden and crisp further as they cool. When they've cooled, finish by seasoning with a sprinkle of salt. These will keep for about 2 weeks in an airtight container on the counter.

ALMOND-CRUSTED ZUCCHINI WEDGES WITH GARLIC + BASIL CASHEW CREAM

2 medium zucchinis

½ teaspoon kosher salt + a sprinkle for the zucchini

1 cup slivered almonds (preferably with no skins), finely chopped

1 cup almond flour

1 teaspoon garlic powder

Freshly ground black pepper

2 large eggs

Extra virgin olive oil for drizzling

½ cup Garlic + Basil Cashew Cream (page 35) for serving

I remember as a kid ordering zucchini sticks at our local Italian restaurant. They were crispy, fried, and served with a side of marinara for dipping. While I still love those zucchini sticks, nowadays, I tend to prefer a lighter, summery version with more nutritious ingredients. The bright flavors of the basil cashew cream are made for this dish, but you can also try different sauces, if you like, to change it up.

Preheat the oven to 400°F.

Slice the zucchinis into wedges by cutting each in half and then slicing each half lengthwise and into three pieces. Line a large plate with paper towels, and place the zucchini on it. Sprinkle some salt evenly over the wedges. Allow it to rest for at least 10 minutes, until you see water being drawn out. Take another piece of paper towel and press down on the zucchini to absorb as much moisture as you can. This will keep them from becoming soggy when you bake them.

In a shallow bowl, mix together the almonds, flour, garlic powder, ½ teaspoon of the salt, and pepper to taste. In a separate shallow bowl, lightly beat the eggs.

Line a baking sheet with parchment and have it nearby. One by one, dip the zucchini wedges into the egg and then into the almond-crust mixture, making sure all sides are evenly coated, and place them onto the baking sheet (see the note on page 149). Do this until all of the wedges are coated. Drizzle the tops with olive oil, and bake for 15 minutes. Remove the baking sheet from the oven, flip the wedges over carefully using tongs, and bake for another 15 minutes. They are done when they are lightly browned and crispy on the outside and fork-tender on the inside. Allow them to cool slightly and serve with the cashew cream.

Note: To coat the zucchini, start with only half of the dry almond mixture in the bowl, to coat half the wedges. Then, add the other half of the mixture to coat the rest of the zucchini. After dipping several wedges you will notice the almond mixture getting moist from the egg, so this allows you to refresh halfway through.

PIRI PIRI BROCCOLI BITES

½ cup chickpea flour

½ cup water

½ teaspoon kosher salt

Freshly ground black pepper

1 head broccoli, cut into florets

⅓ cup sunflower oil (or other high-heat oil)

Piri Piri Sauce (page 34) for serving

I am a big fan of crispy fried veggies, and I am an even bigger fan of making them at home, so I know exactly what it is being used to get them crispy. A batter of chickpea flour and spices, and fried in just a little bit of sunflower oil, is what gives these broccoli florets their crunch. Piri piri sauce adds a spicy zing, but you can also try serving them with other condiments such as Chimichurri + Yogurt (page 32) or Garlic + Basil Cashew Cream (page 35).

———————

Make the batter by mixing together the flour, water, salt, and pepper in a large bowl. Whisk to combine. Toss the broccoli florets in the batter and make sure they are evenly coated.

Line a large plate with paper towel and have it nearby. Heat the oil in a large cast iron pan over medium-high heat. You want to make sure the oil is covering the bottom of the pan, and it should sizzle when you drop in the broccoli. Fry the broccoli for 3 to 5 minutes on each side, until golden brown. Transfer the broccoli to the paper towel–lined plate. You might need to do this in 2 batches because you do not want to crowd the pan. Serve warm with the Piri Piri Sauce on the side.

WARM DRINKS

No matter what the season, you can always find me sipping on some kind of warm beverage throughout the day. Teas are there in the morning to start my day and wake me up, in the afternoon as a little pick-me-up, and again at night when it's time to wind things down. I like the beverages that I drink during the day to be as comforting and nourishing as they are tasty. The following is a collection of the more special warm drink recipes that I often make for myself or for friends.

Lavender Matcha Latte

Serves 1

1 cup cashew, almond, or macadamia milk (page 70)

½ cup water

1 teaspoon matcha green tea powder

Pinch or two of dried lavender

While it might seem a bit unexpected, the floral notes from the lavender play so nicely with the bitter matcha in this lovely latte. This is my morning beverage of choice, and one that I also like to make for friends when they come over for tea. Anyone I have made this for has always been pleasantly surprised by the subtle flavor of the lavender. I typically find dried lavender at my local farm stand in the summer, but you can also source it in some grocery stores or online. When I do find it, I like to stock up. It lasts forever, and a little goes a long way.

Put the milk, water, and matcha in a medium saucepan over medium heat and whisk vigorously to dissolve the matcha and break up any clumps. Add the lavender, bring to a boil, turn the heat to low, and simmer for a couple of minutes. Strain the lavender, or just fish it out using a spoon, and pour the beverage into a mug.

Shiitake Mushroom Tea

Serves 1 to 2

8 ounces dried shiitake mushrooms

1-inch piece ginger, peeled and thinly sliced

1 clove garlic, sliced (optional)

6 cups water

Whenever I feel a cold coming on, I reach for the dried shiitakes I always keep in the pantry and make this very simple, very comforting tea. Mushroom broth is known to have medicinal properties, and besides being so comforting when you are feeling out of sorts, I swear it works wonders in keeping colds at bay.

Put the dried shiitakes, ginger, garlic, if using, and water in a medium saucepan and bring to a simmer over medium heat, then reduce the heat to low. Simmer for at least 1 hour, then ladle just the broth into a mug. I like to leisurely sip on this all day.

Turmeric Ginger Milk
Serves 2

3 cups almond, cashew, or other nondairy milk (page 70)

1-inch piece fresh turmeric, peeled and ground

1-inch piece fresh ginger, peeled and ground

1 tablespoon coconut oil or ghee

1 cinnamon stick

Ground cinnamon to serve

This is my beverage of choice for an afternoon pick-me-up, and besides being warming and tasty, it has incredible antioxidant properties. It is a great drink to make a daily habit of. I find that if I have turmeric every day, I actually feel less achy, it gives me more energy, and I know my insides are loving the anti-inflammatory properties too. You can generally find fresh turmeric root at your local grocery store, near the ginger, or at a health food store. If you cannot source fresh turmeric, you can always substitute one teaspoon of dried ground turmeric.

_____

Put the milk, turmeric, ginger, coconut oil, and cinnamon stick in a medium saucepan and heat over low heat. Do not bring to a boil; you just want to gently simmer to heat the milk. Simmer for 8 to 10 minutes, remove the cinnamon stick, and pour into 2 mugs to serve. Top with a dash of cinnamon and enjoy warm.

Hot Chocolate with Tahini + Cinnamon + Star Anise
Serves 2

3 cups almond, cashew, or other nondairy milk (page 70)

1 tablespoon coconut oil

1 tablespoon tahini

2 ounces good-quality dark chocolate (60%–70% dark), chopped

1 cinnamon stick

2 star anise

This is a super-warming and nourishing beverage for those chillier days. Tahini and chocolate are totally meant to be swirling around together in a warm mug, and spices like cinnamon and star anise add that little extra wonderful. Feel free to add a scoop of coconut whip, or even vanilla ice cream, which would make this more of a dessert or afternoon treat.

_____

Put the milk in a medium saucepan and bring it to a simmer over medium-low heat. Add the coconut oil, tahini, and chocolate, and stir until the chocolate melts. Add the cinnamon stick and star anise, lower the heat, and cook for 8 to 10 minutes. Pour into 2 mugs, and enjoy warm.

THAI PEANUT SWEET POTATO SKINS

3 large sweet potatoes

3 to 4 tablespoons extra virgin olive oil

Sea salt

Freshly ground black pepper

Sweet + Spicy Peanut Sauce
(page 37) for serving

2 scallions, white and light green
parts only, thinly sliced

¼ cup toasted peanuts, almonds,
or cashews

Basil leaves, chiffonade, for serving

Handful of cilantro

These unique potato skins are perfect nibbles to bring to a party or a potluck. It turns out that peanut sauce pairs beautifully with sweet potatoes, and with the addition of nuts, basil, and scallions as toppings, these are crazy delicious. Be sure to reserve the inside of the sweet potato, which can be used as a sweet potato mash or in the Curried Sweet Potato + Yellow Split Pea Stew (page 99).

———————

Preheat the oven to 400°F. Using a fork, poke a bunch of holes in the sweet potatoes. Line a baking sheet with parchment and place the potatoes on it. Bake for 45 minutes to 1 hour, until the sweet potatoes are soft and cooked through.

Remove the sweet potatoes from the oven and set the oven to broil (keep the rack in the middle). Allow the sweet potatoes to rest until they are cool enough to handle. Cut the potatoes in half and scoop out most of the flesh, leaving a thin layer (about ¼ inch) of sweet potato in the skins. Reserve the extra sweet potato flesh for another use. Cut each skin into quarters, brush with the olive oil, season with salt and pepper, and put them back on the parchment-lined baking sheet. Broil for 5 to 7 minutes, turn the potato skins, and broil for another 5 to 7 minutes. You want the edges to be really crispy. Each broiler is different, some cook very fast and others are slow, so keep a close eye on the skins to ensure they don't burn.

Allow the skins to cool slightly before assembling. Add a healthy drizzle of the peanut sauce. Sprinkle the scallions, nuts, basil, and cilantro over the top. Serve warm with extra peanut sauce on the side, for dipping.

SAVORY CRISPY LENTILS + PEPITAS

1 cup cooked black or green lentils

½ cup pepitas (pumpkin seeds)

2 tablespoons extra virgin olive oil

½ teaspoon hot paprika

¼ teaspoon garlic powder

¼ teaspoon sea salt

Freshly ground black pepper

Since I prefer to reach for savory things when I want a snack, I keep this mix around (in lieu of, say, granola), so that I have something crunchy, nutritious, and satisfying to munch on when the mood strikes. This easy-to-make mix also serves as a wonderful topping for soups, salads, or even roasted vegetables.

———————

Preheat the oven to 375°F. Put the lentils and pepitas on a baking sheet, add the olive oil, paprika, garlic powder, salt, and pepper to taste, and toss to coat. Spread them out evenly on the baking sheet. Roast for 10 minutes, give them a shake and stir, and roast for another 10 minutes, or until everything is crunchy and crispy. Enjoy warm out of the oven, or transfer to an airtight container, where it will keep on the counter for about 2 weeks.

MACADAMIA RICOTTA

Special Equipment:
High-powered blender; cheesecloth

1½ cups macadamia nuts, soaked overnight

1 probiotic capsule

1 clove garlic

Juice of ½ lemon (about 1 tablespoon)

½ teaspoon sea salt

¾ cup water

This macadamia ricotta is a dairy-free revelation. As someone who avoids dairy, I find it hard to replicate things like wonderful melty, spreadable cheese, and I am not usually one for foods or recipes that try to fool you into something it is not. With that said, this macadamia ricotta is the closest I have come to homemade dairy-free cheese that is delicious and that acts and tastes like its dairy counterpart. It is perfect to serve as an appetizer at a party, with crackers or veggies, or to use however you would use traditional ricotta; however, the real magic happens when you stuff this in Eggplant Rolls (page 175) and bake them, creating an oozing cheese-like experience.

Put the nuts in the blender, empty the contents of the probiotic capsule (discard the capsule), and add the garlic, lemon juice, salt, and water. Blend on high until very smooth, which might take a couple of minutes, scraping down the sides as needed.

Line a colander with cheesecloth and put the nut mixture on top of the cheesecloth. Place the colander over a bowl, wrap up the edges of the cheesecloth, and place something heavy on top of the wrapped mixture. The weight will allow it to release extra moisture. Leave it on a countertop overnight to ferment. The next day, gather the edges of the cheesecloth, squeeze to release any extra moisture, and transfer the ricotta to an airtight container. Store in the fridge until you're ready to enjoy. This will keep for a few days in the fridge.

SO MANY WAYS TO HUMMUS

I make hummus often, and it's something I keep around for snacking. The type of hummus I make is often determined by what I find in my pantry, and there are so many ways to make hummus outside of the more traditional use of garbanzo beans. One of my favorite bases is lentils, because the earthiness of the lentils lends itself well to other hummus flavors such as lemon and tahini. Veggie-based hummus is fun because you can end up with different colors depending on the veggies that you use. And a much less traditional hummus made with almonds or macadamia nuts is a great way to switch things up, with the nuts adding a touch of sweetness that balances out all the savory elements.

GENERAL RECIPE FOR HUMMUS

Makes 1½ to
2 cups of hummus

Hummus base: lentils, beans, veggies, or nuts

Hummus ingredients (see page 161)

Toppings of your choice

Some ideas for toppings:

- Harissa
- Pesto
- Chimichurri
- Toasted nuts or seeds
- Caramelized onion
- Scallions
- Olives
- Herbs
- Extra virgin olive oil

Put the hummus ingredients in the food processor and process until the mixture is super-smooth, adding additional water (a tablespoon at a time) to thin it out, if needed. Transfer to a bowl and finish with a drizzle of olive oil and your topping of choice.

For the lentil hummus, put ½ cup lentils and 4 cups water into a medium saucepan, bring to a boil, reduce to a simmer, and cook for 45 minutes, or until the lentils are very tender. When the lentils are done cooking, strain, reserving ¼ cup of the cooking water, and transfer them to a food processor with the reserved water and the rest of the hummus ingredients. Follow the rest of the instructions above.

For another variation in flavor, toast your pine nuts and roast your garlic and lemon. For the pine nuts, preheat the oven to 325°F. Line a baking sheet with parchment paper, spread the nuts on it, and toast for about 5 minutes, until golden brown. Let the nuts cool before using.

To roast the garlic and lemon, preheat the oven to 400°F. Separate the garlic into unpeeled cloves and slice the lemon into rounds. Line another baking sheet with parchment paper, place the garlic and lemon on it, and roast them for about 30 minutes, until the garlic is soft and the lemon is charred around the edges. Let them cool before using.

Lentil (green, black, red)

1 cup cooked lentils

+ ¼ cup lentil cooking water

+ 1 clove garlic (raw or roasted)

+ juice from ½ lemon

+ ⅓ cup tahini

+ salt

+ pepper

+ olive oil

Bean (white, black, chickpea)

one 14-ounce can beans of choice, drained and rinsed

+ ¼ cup water

+ 1 clove garlic (raw or roasted)

+ juice from ½ lemon

+ ⅓ cup tahini

+ salt

+ pepper

+ olive oil

Veggie (beet, pea, carrot)

1 cup steamed or roasted veggies

+ ¼ cup water

+ 1 clove garlic (raw or roasted)

+ juice from ½ lemon

+ ⅓ cup tahini

+ salt

+ pepper

+ olive oil

Nut (almond, macadamia nut, walnut)

1 cup skinless nuts, soaked overnight

+ ¼ cup water

+ 1 clove garlic (raw or roasted)

+ juice from ½ lemon or lime

+ ⅓ cup tahini

+ salt

+ pepper

+ olive oil

+ herbs

LEFTOVERS: WRAP IT UP!

Wraps are an ingenious way to enjoy any leftover veggies in the fridge (both cooked and raw), as well as grains and sauces. They're great for a snack or a lunch on the go, one you can eat with your hands. Collards, kale, and nori are the most nutritious as wraps, but there's also rice paper, which I like to think of as more of a treat. These can be stuffed in countless ways. I tend to use nori wraps when I have leftover black or brown rice and some sort of sesame or miso sauce in the fridge. The leafy greens are best stuffed with crunchy raw veggies, or lightly roasted ones with some quinoa for protein, and an herb-forward sauce such as a pesto. Rice paper wraps, which are also used for spring rolls, work best for softer veggies such as roasted sweet potato or avocado. Peanut sauce is my favorite in a rice paper wrap, but experiment with others sauces like chimichurri or even kimchi to add some great punchy flavor.

Big Leafy Green Wraps

Kale or collards, deribbed

Veggies or fruit (raw or lightly roasted): carrots, beets, shiitakes, scallions, celery, cucumbers, tomatoes, zucchini, apples, pears

Herbs: basil, cilantro, parsley

Grains: quinoa, wild rice, brown rice, black rice, millet

Beans or legumes: chickpeas or lentils

Sauces: Pesto (pages 24 to 25), Chimichurri + Yogurt (page 32), Mustard Miso (page 37), Easy One-Pan Romesco Sauce (page 38)

Blanch 2 large leafy greens in water for 1 minute, dunk in an ice bath, and dry on a paper towel. Use two overlapped leaves to wrap, placing 4 to 5 thinly sliced veggies along with any other topping you like—herbs, a grain, a sauce—toward the bottom. Take the bottom of the wrap and fold it up and over the veggies, then fold in the two sides, and roll away from you until it's completely wrapped.

Rice Paper Wraps

Veggies (softer work better): avocado, cucumbers, zucchini, roasted sweet potato or squash, thinly sliced sautéed mushrooms, greens such as spinach, kimchi

Herbs: basil, cilantro, shiso

Nut or seeds: sesame seeds, pumpkin seeds, almonds, peanuts, cashews

Grains (cooked): wild, brown, or white rice

Sauce: Sweet + Spicy Peanut Sauce (page 37), Spicy Ginger Sesame Mustard (page 38), Green Herb Tahini (page 38)

Rehydrate the rice paper wraps by submerging them into a shallow bowl of water for a couple of seconds until they are pliable. Then put the wrap onto a flat surface, and place thinly sliced veggies in the bottom third part of the wrap with any additions and sauces you like. Take the bottom of the wrap and fold it up and over the veggies, then fold in the two sides, and roll away from you until it's completely wrapped.

Nori Wraps

Veggies: avocado, sweet potato, mushrooms, cucumber

Grains (cooked): sushi rice, brown rice, black rice, quinoa

Others: Crispy Shallots (page 30), Garlic Chips (page 30), sesame seeds, cashews, Nori Gomasio (page 31)

Sauces: Spicy Ginger Sesame Mustard (page 38), Mustard Miso (page 31)

Place the nori on a flat surface. Spread the rice out across the sheet of nori, leaving about a 1 inch border on all sides. When working with sushi rice, it can be easier to spread if you keep your fingertips moist with water. Place any veggies, sauce, or other additions in the center, and either roll the nori into a cone shape, or fold up the two sides and eat like a taco.

VEGGIE
ENTREES

Even though I am not vegetarian, I really believe that everyone can benefit from incorporating more vegetable-based meals into their weekly routine. When I started cooking with more vegetables and less meat and dairy, I became fascinated by the possibilities in paring down recipes and thinking more creatively about utilizing available vegetables, grains, and legumes. It's all about making the most of the gorgeous produce that is in season and can be found in your backyard, at the farm stands, at the farmers' markets, or in the grocery store. The seasonal component of cooking with vegetables is my favorite part of vegetarian cooking—it makes meals feel more celebratory and signals when it is time for us to change up our cooking techniques. Vegetables announce that spring is here when we see an abundance of greens at the farmers' market. I get so excited when tomatoes are plentiful, ripe, and juicy—a sign that summer has hit its peak. Root vegetables in the winter tell us it's time for stews, braised dishes, and warming meals by the fireplace. Vegetables are best when they are allowed to shine, and you will find that the simple recipes in this chapter reflect that more-with-less philosophy.

VEGGIE ENTREES

Olive Oil Baked Chickpeas with Lemon + Garlic + Shallots   170

Garlic + Lemon Marinated Artichokes with Quinoa Pilaf   172

Eggplant Rolls Stuffed with Macadamia Ricotta + Roasted Tomato Pesto   175

Ratatouille Pot Pie with a Potato Crust   176

Quinoa + Mushroom + Beet Burgers with Chimichurri   179

Crispy Cauliflower Steaks with Ginger Scallion Sauce   180

Turmeric Spice Rubbed Roasted Carrots + Harissa Polenta   183

Harissa + Coconut Milk Baked Delicata Squash with Lentils + Toasted Almonds   184

Oven-Baked Risotto Rice with Kale + Leek + Mushrooms   187

Crisp Sautéed Maitake Mushrooms with Nori Miso Butter   188

Roasted Beets + Butternut Squash with Beluga Lentils + Tarragon Salsa Verde   191

Coconut Curry Lentilballs   192

Vegetables Mains (Six Ways)

Eggplant or Zucchini   194

Delicata or Acorn Squash   194

Red Peppers   195

Sweet Potato   195

Portobella Mushroom   195

Leeks   195

OLIVE OIL BAKED CHICKPEAS WITH LEMON + GARLIC + SHALLOTS

Special Equipment:
9 x 5-inch loaf pan or baking dish

Two 14-ounce cans chickpeas, rinsed

6 cloves garlic, peeled and smashed

5 shallots, peeled and quartered

1 lemon, deseeded and thinly sliced

½ teaspoon kosher salt

½ teaspoon paprika

2 sprigs fresh oregano

2 sprigs rosemary

1 cup extra virgin olive oil

Baguette, rice, or quinoa for serving

These super-flavorful, one-dish braised chickpeas can be served so many ways—as an appetizer for dipping with some crusty bread, as a side dish, or as dinner all by itself over some rice or quinoa. If you're lucky enough to have leftovers, they are even better the next day.

_____

Preheat the oven to 375°F. Put the chickpeas, garlic, shallots, lemon, salt, paprika, oregano, and rosemary into the baking dish, and cover with 1 cup of olive oil. If most of the ingredients are not submerged in the oil, add a little more. They should be submerged at least ¾ of the way. Cover with aluminum foil, and bake for about 40 minutes. Serve warm with some toasted bread or over rice or quinoa, or as a salad topper. This will keep for about a week in an airtight container in the fridge.

GARLIC + LEMON MARINATED ARTICHOKES
WITH QUINOA PILAF

Artichokes

3 globe artichokes

½ cup extra virgin olive oil

5 cloves garlic, pressed

Juice from 2 lemons

Sea salt

Freshly ground black pepper

Red pepper flakes (optional)

Quinoa Pilaf

1 cup quinoa

2 cups water

Sea salt

Drizzle of extra virgin olive oil

Squeeze of lemon juice

⅓ cup toasted almonds or pine nuts

¼ cup chopped parsley

5 to 7 basil leaves, chopped

To Serve

Miso Butter (page 27) or Basil Cilantro Aioli (page 121)

Anyone who knows me well knows of my deep love for artichokes. They were a special afterschool snack for me as a kid, and steamed artichokes were one of the first recipes I tackled in college. As I became braver and more experimental in the kitchen, I came up with new ideas for artichoke recipes, and these marinated, stuffed artichokes have become my favorite way to prepare them. While the marinating requires a little extra time and work, this is a great make-ahead kind of meal. You can steam and marinate the artichokes on the weekend, and even prepare the pilaf ahead of time, and then eat them throughout the week at your leisure while any extras continue marinating in the fridge. You can also skip the marinating or the pilaf and serve these simply grilled with a side of butter or aioli.

Artichokes

Slice off the top half of the artichokes, but keep the stems intact. Using scissors, snip off the tops of the leaves where the prickly bits are. Place a large pot of water with a steamer basket over high heat (make sure the water comes up to the basket but does not go over) and bring to a boil. Place the artichokes in the steamer basket, cover, and steam for 30 minutes, until a leaf can be easily removed. Remove them from the pot and allow them to cool slightly.

While the artichokes are steaming, prepare the marinade. Place the olive oil, garlic, lemon juice, pinch of salt, black pepper and red pepper flakes to taste, if using, in a large, shallow bowl or baking dish. When the artichokes have cooled, slice them down the center.

Using a spoon, scoop out the prickly insides that surround the heart. Put the artichokes in the bowl or dish with the marinade and make sure to coat all sides in the marinade. Cover, and put them in the fridge until you are ready to serve. It is best to marinate them overnight or for a day, but if you don't have the time you can marinade them for 20 to 30 minutes (or skip it altogether). You can keep them marinating for a few days if you like.

Quinoa Pilaf

Put the quinoa, water, and salt in a medium saucepan, bring to a boil, cover, reduce to a simmer, and cook for 15 minutes. Remove from the heat, add the olive oil, lemon juice, nuts, parsley, and basil, and cover again while you're grilling the artichokes.

Grill and Serve

Heat up the grill or a grill pan to medium-high. Place the artichokes cut side down and grill for about 5 minutes on each side.

To serve, place the artichokes on a plate, cut side up. Fill the cavity near the heart with the quinoa pilaf, and serve with miso butter or aioli, or the dipping sauce of your choice, on the side (to dip the leaves).

EGGPLANT ROLLS STUFFED WITH MACADAMIA RICOTTA + ROASTED TOMATO PESTO

Special Equipment:
8 x 8-inch baking dish

2 medium eggplants

4 to 5 tablespoons extra virgin olive oil

Sea salt

Freshly ground black pepper

1 cup Roasted Tomato Pesto (page 25) or jarred tomato sauce

1 cup Macadamia Ricotta (page 158)

Handful of basil leaves, coarsely chopped

When I was growing up, my mom claimed that my favorite food was eggplant rollatini. I actually think it was her favorite food and she was just training me to like it as much as she did so she could make it all the time. In any case, I did end up loving eggplant (a lot), and I've always wanted to come up with a dairy-free version of my mom's beloved meal. The macadamia ricotta that these eggplant rolls are stuffed with blows me away. It is one of the best substitutes I have found for that real cheese-like experience in a meal such as this. If you don't want to take the extra steps to make the macadamia ricotta, you can also use a store-bought dairy-free ricotta or even a regular ricotta. Or, as another dairy-free alternative, stuff these rolls with some steamed rice and spinach.

Preheat the oven to 400°F. Slice the eggplant lengthwise into ⅛-inch-thick pieces. Line a large baking sheet with parchment and put the eggplant on it, brush each side generously and evenly with olive oil, and season with salt and pepper. Bake for 10 to 15 minutes, until the eggplant is soft and pliable enough to roll.

Pour half of the tomato pesto into the bottom of the baking dish. Place the eggplant lengthwise on a flat surface, then place a dollop of the ricotta and smear it to cover the piece of eggplant, reserving a little room around the edges. Roll each eggplant up, away from you, and place it in the baking dish. Do this until all of the remaining eggplant slices are stuffed, then spoon the remaining tomato pesto over the eggplant. Return the rolls to the oven for another 20 minutes, or until everything is oozing and the tops of the eggplant look toasted. Allow to cool for a few minutes before serving. Sprinkle with basil leaves. This can be made a few hours ahead and kept covered in the fridge, reserving the last step in the oven until you're ready to serve.

RATATOUILLE POT PIE WITH A POTATO CRUST

Special Equipment:
9-inch round baking dish

3 to 4 medium white potatoes, thinly sliced

3 to 4 tablespoons extra virgin olive oil

1 medium-size eggplant, diced

1 large onion, diced

5 cloves garlic, smashed and thinly sliced

Pinch or two of red pepper flakes

½ teaspoon kosher salt

Freshly ground black pepper

1 medium zucchini, diced

1 medium yellow zucchini, diced

1 pint grape tomatoes, cut in half

⅓ cup white wine or mirin

5 to 6 basil leaves, finely chopped

I eat veggies as a main dish at least a few times a week, and I love to make this ratatouille pot pie with a crispy potato crust when the late summer veggies are at their prime. I use vegetables that you can still find out of season, so you could easily make this filling main dish well into the winter. It's a great way to feed a crowd, but don't be afraid to make this for two—the leftovers are even better the next day.

———————

Preheat the oven to 425°F. Using about half of the sliced potatoes, make a single layer at the bottom of the baking dish, drizzle lightly with olive oil, and set aside while you make the ratatouille.

Heat 2 tablespoons of the oil in a large, deep pan over medium heat. Add the eggplant and cook for about 10 minutes, until lightly browned and tender. If the eggplant has absorbed all the oil, add more so it does not stick to the bottom of the pan. Remove the eggplant and set aside. In the same pan, add a little more oil and the onion. Cook for 5 to 7 minutes, until the onion is soft and starting to brown. Then add the garlic, red pepper flakes, salt, and pepper to taste and cook for 2 minutes. Add both zucchini, and cook for about 10 minutes, until soft, and add in the tomatoes. Cook for another 5 or so minutes, then add back the eggplant. Add the wine and cook for a few minutes, until about half of the liquid has evaporated and all of the vegetables are tender and cooked through. At this point you should have a little bit of "sauce" from the vegetables and wine left at the bottom of the pan. Add the basil, give it a stir to incorporate, and remove it from the heat and pour the ratatouille into the baking dish.

Layer the remaining potatoes over the top, brush the potatoes generously with olive oil, and season with salt and pepper. Bake for 30 minutes, or until the potatoes are browned around the edges and tender. Allow to cool for a few minutes before serving. Serve warm.

QUINOA + MUSHROOM + BEET BURGERS WITH CHIMICHURRI

1 cup cooked and cooled quinoa

2 small scrubbed and cubed beets (about 1 cup)

2 cups roughly chopped shiitake mushrooms

3 scallions, white and light green parts only, chopped

1 large clove garlic, minced

½ teaspoon sea salt

Freshly ground black pepper

⅓ cup rolled oats

⅓ cup sunflower seeds

2 eggs, lightly beaten

2 tablespoons vegetable oil

Hamburger buns or lettuce leaves for serving

Chimichurri + Yogurt (page 32)

While I definitely prefer homemade veggie burgers, I don't always love how labor-intensive some recipes can be. These flavorful burgers are my weeknight go-to—they are so easy to make, because all you have to do is chop the veggies, add them to a food processor, and form the mixture into veggie patties. You'll find that the beet and mushroom combination pack in so much "meatiness," which is exactly how I want my veggies burger to be.

———————

Put the quinoa, beets, mushrooms, scallions, garlic, salt, and pepper to taste in a food processor and pulse until everything is chopped and uniform with no chunks, scraping down the sides as needed. Add the oats and pulse again to incorporate. Add the sunflower seeds and pulse just a couple of times. Transfer the mixture to a bowl, and stir in the eggs. Place the mixture in the fridge for at least 30 minutes or longer if you prefer to do this a day or two in advance.

Remove the mixture from the fridge, and form into 4 or 5 patties. Heat the vegetable oil in a cast iron pan over medium heat and cook the patties for about 5 minutes on each side, until browned. Do this 2 patties at a time so as to not crowd the pan, until all of the patties are cooked. Serve on buns or in lettuce wraps, topped with a generous smear of the chimichurri, along with any other toppings you choose.

CRISPY CAULIFLOWER STEAKS WITH GINGER SCALLION SAUCE

1 large head cauliflower

1 cup chickpea flour

1 cup water

1 teaspoon garlic powder

½ teaspoon sea salt

Freshly ground black pepper

2 tablespoons grapeseed oil
+ more for frying florets

Ginger Scallion Sauce (page 37) for serving

Inspired by crispy, crunchy, buffalo cauliflower—an indulgent veggie treat—I decided to create a version using a whole cauliflower steak. When cutting the cauliflower into "steaks," it's best to start from the middle and work your way out. Depending on the size of your cauliflower, you might only get two steaks per cauliflower before the ends start to fall apart into florets, so it is best to choose the largest cauliflower you can find. I toss the florets from the ends of the cauliflower in the remaining batter and fry them once the steaks are done, and serve them on top or on the side of the larger steak. Alternatively, you can reserve the extra cauliflower florets and use them in a soup or salad.

———

Trim the green leaves off the bottom of the cauliflower, and place it on a cutting board stem side down. Slice the cauliflower down the center, then again through each half, making sure each steak is about ½ inch thick. Repeat until the steaks no longer hold together. You should end up with 2 whole steaks, but you might be able to get 1 or 2 additional steaks out of the cauliflower. Break up the remaining cauliflower pieces into florets and set aside, or store for later use.

In a large, shallow bowl, whisk together the chickpea flour, water, garlic powder, salt, and pepper to taste. Heat the oil in a large cast iron pan over medium heat. Dip one of the steaks into the batter and flip it to coat it evenly. Transfer the steak from the bowl to the pan, and cook for 3 to 5 minutes on each side, until golden brown. Do this until all the steaks are cooked. If you want to cook the florets as well, add another tablespoon of oil to the pan, toss all the remaining florets in the batter, and fry them, turning every couple of minutes, until golden brown and cooked all over. Serve warm with a spoonful of the ginger scallion sauce on top.

TURMERIC SPICE RUBBED ROASTED CARROTS + HARISSA POLENTA

½ cup Carrot Top Harissa (page 32)

2 cloves garlic

1 teaspoon turmeric

1 teaspoon cumin

½ teaspoon cinnamon

1½ teaspoon kosher salt

Pinch of cayenne

¼ cup extra virgin olive oil

10 medium carrots, cleaned and trimmed

6 cups water

1 cup polenta

One day I accidentally added harissa to polenta, and it turned out to be a wonderful mistake. I could not believe how well the flavors of the harissa went with this super-creamy polenta. If you have made polenta but have had a hard time getting it creamy without cream or butter, the trick is to add a lot of water—six times the amount of polenta in order to get really creamy (creamless) polenta. Feel free to switch out other veggies for the carrots, or throw in additional ones. Sweet potato or squash would work great with the carrots or on their own.

———————

Make the harissa first if you do not have it prepared already.

Preheat the oven to 400°F.

Put the garlic, turmeric, cumin, cinnamon, salt, cayenne, and olive oil in a food processor and blend until a smooth paste forms. Put the carrots on a baking sheet and rub with the spice mixture. Roast for about 30 minutes, until the carrots are soft and browning.

While the carrots are roasting, make the polenta. Heat the water in a medium saucepan over medium-high heat, and slowly pour in the polenta while stirring (the water does not need to be boiling). Continue stirring for about 2 minutes, until it starts to thicken slightly. Turn the heat to low, and set the timer for 30 minutes. You will want to stir your polenta every few minutes to make sure it's not sticking on the bottom. After 30 minutes, the polenta should be smooth and creamy. Add a little more water if you find it is too thick. Then, drizzle in the harissa, stir, cover the pot, and remove from the heat until you're ready to serve. Also, if you're making this ahead of time, let the polenta sit, covered; to warm up just add a little water, and stir it over low heat. To serve, spread the warm polenta out on a plate and place the carrots on top.

HARISSA + COCONUT MILK BAKED DELICATA SQUASH WITH LENTILS + TOASTED ALMONDS

2 medium Delicata squashes,
deseeded and
sliced into half moons

1 large red onion, cut into wedges

¼ cup harissa

½ cup lentils

One 13½-ounce can full-fat
coconut milk

¼ cup water

⅓ cup toasted almonds

Handful of chopped herbs
(cilantro, basil, parsley)

In this one-pan vegetarian dinner the lentils get cooked in the pan with the coconut milk and harissa; with the added squash you end up with a luscious, flavorful, and fulfilling meal for a quiet night at home or as a holiday side dish. If you do not have harissa handy, you could also use a curry paste of your choice. And if you cannot find Delicata squash, you can use any kind of squash or a sweet potato—just make sure you peel the outer edges if you're using a hard-skinned squash.

———————

Preheat the oven to 425°F. Put the squash, onion, and harissa in a medium, deep baking dish, toss, and bake for 20 to 25 minutes, until the vegetables are tender. Remove from the oven, sprinkle the lentils evenly over the vegetables, and pour the coconut milk and water over the top, making sure the lentils are submerged. Return to the oven and cook for another 30 to 35 minutes, until the lentils are cooked. Top with the toasted almonds and herbs, and serve warm.

OVEN-BAKED RISOTTO RICE WITH KALE + LEEK + MUSHROOMS

2 tablespoons extra virgin olive oil

1 large leek, sliced

2 cups mushrooms (shiitake, oyster), sliced

2 cups chopped kale

1 clove garlic, minced

1 teaspoon kosher salt

Freshly ground black pepper

1 cup Arborio rice

½ cup dry white wine

2 cups hot water

2 tablespoons unsalted butter or 2 additional tablespoons extra virgin olive oil

Chopped chives or parsley for serving (optional)

Pesto for serving (pages 24 to 25; optional)

While I am a big fan of traditional risotto, this recipe is more of a shortcut—a much easier version of a regular risotto when you have a craving but don't want to stand over a pot stirring for thirty-plus minutes. Oven-baking risotto rice will not give you the same creamy consistency, but it is nonetheless very delicious, serves several people, and makes great leftovers. Feel free to play around with different vegetable combinations here besides the kale, leek, and mushrooms. Other greens such as Swiss chard or spinach would be great instead of kale, and you could also switch out mushrooms for eggplant, cauliflower, or zucchini—just note that you'll need to increase their sauté time slightly.

———————

Preheat the oven to 350°F.

In a heavy-bottomed pot, heat the oil over medium heat, and add the leek. Cook for a couple of minutes, until the leeks are translucent. Add the mushrooms and cook for 2 to 3 minutes. Add the kale and cook for a couple of minutes, until it's wilted. Add the garlic and cook for another 2 minutes, then add the salt and pepper to taste.

Add the rice to the pot and cook for a couple of minutes. Add the wine and cook until it's almost completely evaporated, about 7 to 10 minutes. Add the hot water and butter or olive oil, cover, and put the pot in the oven for 15 minutes. Remove the pot from the oven and check to make sure all the water has been absorbed. Give it a stir and then transfer to a large serving bowl or individual serving dishes. Top with chopped chives, parsley, or pesto, if using, and serve.

CRISP SAUTÉED MAITAKE MUSHROOMS
WITH NORI MISO BUTTER

2 tablespoons grapeseed oil
(or other neutral high-heat oil)

4 maitake (hen of the woods)
mushrooms

2 tablespoons Nori Miso Butter
(page 27)

Sea salt

Freshly ground black pepper

I like to think of maitake mushrooms as the steak of vegetable world. They are meaty and so flavorful—especially when sautéed until tender and crisp. They can be a little tricky to find, but you can usually source them in a grocery store with a great mushroom selection, or at farmers' markets. If you cannot find maitake mushrooms (also known as hen of the woods), you can also make this with the more commonly found portobella mushroom. These mushrooms with some spinach and rice or quinoa make a great vegetarian dinner.

Heat the oil in a cast iron pan over medium-high heat. Add the mushrooms and cook for 4 or 5 minutes, without disturbing too much (so that is has the chance to get a nice char), then flip and cook for another 4 or 5 minutes on the other side. When there is about 2 minutes left, add the nori miso butter and toss to coat the mushrooms, then season with salt and pepper. Transfer to a plate, and serve warm.

ROASTED BEETS + BUTTERNUT SQUASH WITH BELUGA LENTILS + TARRAGON SALSA VERDE

1 small butternut squash, peeled, deseeded, and cubed or sliced into wedges

4 beets, scrubbed and sliced into wedges

1 large red onion, cut into wedges

2 tablespoons extra virgin olive oil

Sea salt

Freshly ground black pepper

1 cup beluga lentils or green lentils, rinsed

4 cups water

¼ cup sunflower seeds (toasted, if you prefer)

About ½ cup Tarragon Salsa Verde (page 34)

Here are a few other wonderful veggie bowl combinations to try:

- Sweet Potato + Red Onion
- Eggplant + Zucchini
- Cauliflower + Fennel
- Artichokes + Asparagus
- Carrots + Shiitakes

There are many nights when I am quite content to have a bowl full of veggies and a grain, legume, or rice doused in a flavorful sauce, especially when I am feeding only myself—it's quick, nourishing, and delicious. This recipe is a slightly elevated version of what one of those humble weeknight meals would look like. Beets, butternut squash, and red onions are a wonderful, colorful, flavorful trio, and the lentils make this bowl of simple roasted veggies feel more like a substantial meal.

Preheat the oven to 400°F. Place the squash, beets, and onion on a large baking sheet, drizzle with the olive oil, and season with salt and pepper. Roast for 30 to 40 minutes, until tender.

While the veggies are roasting, make the lentils. Put the lentils in a pot with the water, bring to a boil, reduce to a simmer, and cook for 25 minutes, or until the lentils are tender and cooked but still have a slight bite to them. Drain and put in a serving bowl with the sunflower seeds. When they are done roasting, add the squash, beets, and onion to the bowl and toss to combine. Transfer to individual serving plates or bowls and drizzle the salsa verde on top.

COCONUT CURRY LENTILBALLS

Lentilballs

1 cup cooked green or black lentils

1 cup shiitakes, sliced

2 scallions, white and light green parts only, minced

1 clove garlic, minced

1 teaspoon ground coriander

½ teaspoon sea salt

Freshly ground black pepper

¼ cup rolled oats

¼ cup pine nuts

1 large egg

2 to 3 tablespoons grapeseed oil (or other neutral high-heat oil)

Coconut Curry

1 tablespoon grapeseed oil (or other neutral high-heat oil)

1 medium yellow onion, diced (about 2 cups)

1 clove garlic, minced

One 13½-ounce can light or full-fat coconut milk

3 tablespoons curry paste (I like yellow curry, but red and green are both delicious)

Squeeze of lime juice

2 handfuls of fresh chopped herbs (cilantro, parsley, or basil)

I know there are lots of lentil "meatball" recipes out there, but these—swimming in a spicy, creamy coconut curry sauce—are the dreamiest ones I've ever eaten. So many of the vegetarian meatballs I have tried are on the dry side, so I went on a mission to create one that is moist, flavorful, and easy enough to be thrown together for a weeknight meal. The shiitakes keep the meatballs super-moist, and the coconut curry makes them really flavorful. I either serve these all on their own (since the lentils are so hearty and filling) or spoon them with their sauce over some rice or quinoa. If you love these as much as I do, make a double batch and freeze any extras for a later use.

———

Lentilballs

Put the lentils, shiitakes, scallions, garlic, coriander, salt, pepper, oats, pine nuts, and egg in a food processor and pulse several times until the ingredients are incorporated. Take a small handful of the mixture (a little more than 1 tablespoon) and roll it between the palms of your hands. Place it on a plate. Do this until all of the lentilballs have been formed.

Heat the oil in a large, deep frying pan over medium heat. Add the lentilballs and brown on each side, about 10 minutes total. Transfer back to the plate and set aside while you prepare the curry.

Curry

Add 1 tablespoon or so of oil, if necessary, to the same frying pan and add the onion. Cook for 5 to 7 minutes, until soft, then add the garlic and cook for another 2 minutes, until fragrant. Add the coconut milk, curry paste, and lime juice, and stir to dissolve the curry paste. Add the lentilballs to the curry, and cook for another 5 minutes. Sprinkle the herbs over the top, and serve warm.

VEGETABLE MAINS (SIX WAYS)

Often on weeknights when I want something quick and healthy, I throw a veggie into the oven to roast, then stuff and top it with things that I find in the fridge, or whatever is simple and nutritious to whip up, such as some rice or quinoa, toasted nuts, and seeds. The following are some easy vegetarian ideas for main meals that are a flash to throw together and are totally flexible, depending on what you have available to you.

For all of these dishes, preheat the oven to 400°F. Slice the veggies in half, drizzle with olive oil, season with salt and pepper, and roast until tender, usually 20 to 40 minutes, depending on the vegetable. Then stuff and finish with the toppings you like, and serve.

Eggplant or Zucchini
Serves 2

(stuffed with)
Hummus (page 160) or
Macadamia Ricotta (page 158)

———

Tomato + Shallot + Garlic Confit (page 25) or
Tomato + Cucumber Salad (page 68) or
Olive Oil Baked Chickpeas (page 170)

———

(topped with)
Nori Gomasio (page 31) or
Crispy Shallots (page 30)

Delicata or Acorn Squash
Serves 2

(stuffed with)
wild rice or quinoa

———

pumpkim seeds + raisins + walnuts or almonds

———

(topped with)
Garlic + Basil Cashew Cream (page 35) or
Carrot Top Harissa (page 32) or
Tarragon Salsa Verde (page 34) or
Ginger Scallion Sauce (page 37)

Red Peppers
Serves 2

(stuffed with)

lentils + mushrooms + Swiss chard or spinach

_____

(topped with)

any kind of pesto (pages 24 to 25)

Sweet Potato
Serves 2

(stuffed with)

sautéed spinach + white bean + quinoa

_____

(topped with)

Green Herb Tahini (page 38) or
Chimichurri + Yogurt (page 32) or
Hazelnut or Pumpkin Seed Dukkah (page 29)

Portobella Mushroom
Serves 2

(stuffed with)

Lentil Hummus (page 161) or
Olive Oil Baked Chickpeas (page 170)

_____

(topped with)

Easy One-Pan Romesco Sauce (page 38) or
Kale + Olive Pesto (page 24) + Crispy Shallots (page 30) or
Garlic Chips (page 30)

Leeks
Serves 2

(stuffed with)

quinoa or
millet or wild rice

_____

toasted nuts or seeds

_____

(topped with)

Easy One-Pan Romesco Sauce (page 38) or
Everyday Shallot + Mustard Vinaigrette (page 39)

FISH

I spend a lot of my time in a little beach town in Long Island, New York, called Amagansett. Fresh seafood is a part of our culture there, so we know what is in season and what is freshest each month. We eat seafood most often in the summertime when the scallops and black bass are at their freshest and make it to our plate the same day they are harvested or caught.

When choosing what fish to bring home and cook, there are a few things that are good to consider. First, I always like to look for fish that is wild-caught. With wild-caught fish you know that you are getting the most nutrient-dense piece of fish without having to worry about questionable farming practices. I also like to know if the seafood I am purchasing is sustainably caught; sometimes this will be labeled, or you can always ask the person behind the counter. Lastly, I always like to consider fish that are low in mercury, and a good rule of thumb is that the smaller the fish—or the higher up it swims—the better. The best thing is to find a seafood shop that you trust and become friendly with the people who work there—chances are they care about these things too and will be happy to help you make the best choices.

Seafood is best when it is done simply, without a lot of steps or preparation. Here are a few of my foolproof recipes, perfect for when you want an easy, healthy, elegant meal.

FISH

Olive Oil Poached Fish   200

Crispy Skinned Black Sea Bass
with Olive + Basil Tapenade   203

Green Curry Fish Stew   204

Sesame Seared Salmon with Crispy
Rice Cakes + Spicy Ginger Sesame
Mustard   206

Lentil + Tomato + Olive Baked Cod
with Lemon Caper Vinaigrette   208

Crispy Cornmeal-Dusted Scallops
with Chimichurri   211

Whole Roasted Fish with Tarragon Salsa
Verde   212

Slow-Cooked Salmon Niçoise
Platter   215

Almond-Crusted Fish Tacos with Quick
Pickled Chilies + Avocado Mash   216

Quick One-Pan Meals = Fish + Veggies

Cod + Eggplant, Tomatoes,
and Garlic   218

Halibut + Squash, Shallots,
and Pesto   219

Salmon + Broccoli and Spicy
Ginger Sesame Mustard   219

Coconut Curry Sea Bass +
Sweet Potatoes and Red
Onion   219

Maple Mustard Miso Marinated
Black Cod   221

Turmeric Garlic-Rubbed Fish in
Parchment   222

OLIVE OIL POACHED FISH

Special Equipment:
A small but deep frying pan, big enough to hold the amount of fish you are using but not too big, or else you waste precious olive oil.

Two 8-ounce pieces of fish
(any kind, including shellfish)

Sea salt

Freshly ground black pepper

2 cups extra virgin olive oil (depending on how much fish you are cooking and pan size)

Add-ins for the oil (garlic, lemon, or chilies)

Vegetables or rice for serving

This is the easiest, tastiest, and healthiest way to enjoy any kind of fish or shellfish, but even more so on a busy weeknight when you want something quick to eat. Olive oil poaching might sound like a complicated method, but it is actually such a simple way to cook fish quickly while retaining its moisture and flavor. If you want to get creative, add such things as garlic, lemon, and chilies to flavor the oil, and after you're done poaching, you can use the leftover oil to drizzle over veggies, rice, or bread.

————————

Pat your fish dry with a piece of paper towel, and season with salt and pepper. Place the fish in the pan (see note in Special Equipment), and cover with enough olive oil so it comes about halfway up the sides of the fish. Add any other flavors, such as garlic, lemon, or chilies, that you wish. Place the pan over low heat. Cook, while basting often, for 20 to 30 minutes, until the fish is opaque and cooked to your liking. Reserve the olive oil and spoon it over vegetables or rice you might be serving with it, or in a bowl for dipping.

CRISPY SKINNED BLACK SEA BASS WITH OLIVE + BASIL TAPENADE

Special Equipment:
Fish spatula

Two 6- to 8-ounce fillets
black sea bass, with skin

Sea salt

Freshly ground black pepper

1 tablespoon extra virgin olive oil

2 tablespoons ghee or
unsalted butter

⅓ cup white wine

Juice of ½ lemon
(about 1 tablespoon)

Olive + Basil Tapenade
(page 39) for serving

Knowing how to get perfectly crisp skin on a fish is a skill that someone who likes to cook fish at home should know how to do. It is not hard, but it does take a little care and finesse, which I outline in the instructions below. If you like, you can also try serving this fish with a pesto (pages 24 to 25) or Chimichurri (page 32, without the optional yogurt).

About 30 minutes before searing the fish, remove it from the refrigerator and place each fillet between two pieces of paper towel to draw out any excess moisture. Season both sides of the fish with salt and pepper.

Heat a medium frying pan over medium-high heat, and add the olive oil and 1 tablespoon of ghee. Place one fillet in the pan, skin side down. When the fish hits the pan, it will likely puff up. Using a fish spatula or regular spatula, apply firm pressure until the fish lies flat again. Once the fish is lying flat, add the second piece and follow the same instructions. Cook each fillet for 3 to 4 minutes, until cooked almost all the way through (nearly opaque). Flip the fish, being careful not to tear the skin, and cook for 1 more minute. Remove from the pan and set aside on a plate.

Add the wine to the pan to deglaze, scraping the bottom of the pan to remove remaining bits of cooked fish, and cook until is has reduced by two-thirds. Add the remaining tablespoon of ghee and the lemon juice and stir. Remove from the heat, and spoon the sauce over the fish. Finish with a spoonful of the tapenade over each fillet and serve immediately.

GREEN CURRY FISH STEW

2 tablespoons grapeseed oil (or other neutral oil)

1 small onion, diced (about 1½ cups)

1 medium zucchini, chopped

1 clove garlic, minced

Sea salt

¼ cup green curry paste

Handful of bok choy or spinach, trimmed and roughly chopped

One 13½-ounce can full-fat coconut milk

1 cup water or vegetable broth

1 pound halibut or monkfish

2 cups steamed rice

Handful of chopped cilantro

Several basil leaves, torn

1 jalapeño, thinly sliced (optional)

This flavorful weeknight dinner ends up being faster to throw together than it is getting Thai food delivered. It is a standby when I am craving those fresh, bright Thai curry flavors. Other veggies can be added to this, or switched out, depending on what you have on hand. Corn, cherry tomatoes, or Swiss chard would all make great additions.

———

Heat the oil in a heavy-bottomed pot over medium heat. Add the onion, cook for 2 minutes, then add the zucchini and cook for 8 to 10 minutes, until all of the veggies are soft and the zucchini is starting to brown around the edges. Add the garlic, season with salt, and cook for another 2 minutes. Add the curry paste, and stir to coat the ingredients. Add the bok choy, stir for about 1 minute, until it wilts slightly, and add the coconut milk and water. Add the fish and simmer for 8 to 10 minutes, until the fish is opaque. Ladle the soup into bowls over some rice, or serve the rice on the side and add it as you wish. Top with the cilantro, basil, and jalapeño, if using.

SESAME SEARED SALMON WITH CRISPY RICE CAKES + SPICY GINGER SESAME MUSTARD

Crispy Rice Cakes

1 cup cooked sushi rice

¼ teaspoon sea salt

2 tablespoons brown rice vinegar

2 tablespoons sunflower oil
(or other neutral high-heat oil)

Sesame Salmon

1 egg white

Two 8-ounce pieces wild salmon

1 cup black and/or white sesame seeds

Sea salt

Freshly ground black pepper

2 tablespoons sunflower oil
(or other high-heat oil)

To Serve

Spicy Ginger Sesame Mustard
(page 38)

There is something about crispy, crunchy rice that feels like an indulgent treat. And, the best accompaniment to crispy rice is a seared piece of salmon and some spicy ginger mustard to dip it all in. This is my perfect weeknight meal, and it's great when you are craving something special but healthy. Of course, if you just want to make the sesame salmon, you can serve it on its own or with regular rice and a side of sautéed greens.

Crispy Rice Cakes

Have a small bowl with water nearby to keep your fingers wet while preparing the rice cakes, to prevent the rice from sticking. Mix the rice with the salt and vinegar. Take a large spoonful of rice and press it together firmly with your fingers to form a rectangle (similar in shape to the piece of salmon). Do this until you have 4 rectangles.

Add the oil to a large cast iron pan, enough so that it covers the bottom of the pan, and heat over medium-high heat. Cook the rice cakes for 3 to 5 minutes on each side, until golden brown, and transfer to a serving plate. You might have to do this in 2 rounds, and if so, allow the pan to cool down slightly, wipe out any excess rice bits, and add some more oil. This will prevent the rice cakes from burning.

Sesame Salmon

Brush a thin layer of egg white over the tops and sides of the salmon, sprinkle the sesame seeds all over, and season with salt and pepper. Using the same cast iron pan as the rice cakes, heat the oil over medium-high heat. Once the pan is hot—you want the salmon to sizzle when it hits the pan—add the salmon skin side up and cook for about 5 minutes. Flip the salmon and cook for another 8 to 10 minutes. I prefer to cook my salmon to medium rare, but if you want it to be well done, cook for a little longer. It's done when the sides are cooked through and it easily flakes apart. You can usually flake apart the layers to see how done the salmon is without having to make a cut down the middle.

Place the salmon on top of the rice cakes, and spoon the ginger mustard over the top.

LENTIL + TOMATO + OLIVE BAKED COD
WITH LEMON CAPER VINAIGRETTE

Special Equipment:
9 x 9-inch baking dish

½ cup black lentils

1 pint cherry tomatoes, halved

½ cup Kalamata olives, halved

3 scallions, white and light green
parts only, thinly sliced

1 lemon, thinly sliced

1½ cups Vegetable Broth
(page 108) or water

Four to six 6-ounce fillets
cod (or other thick white fish),
skin removed

Sea salt

Freshly ground black pepper

Lemon Caper Vinaigrette
(page 40) for serving

It is always great to have a couple of impressive dinner dishes that you can throw together for a party or to feed a crowd without having to do a lot of dishes. This baked fish recipe is perfect for an impromptu gathering. It's basically a one-dish meal—everything (including cooking the lentils) is done in one pan. You can switch up the cod for whatever fish is local and in season, keeping in mind the cooking time might change depending on the thickness of the fish, so check the fish accordingly while cooking.

———————

Preheat the oven to 400°F. Put the lentils, tomatoes, olives, scallions, and lemon into the baking dish and pour the vegetable broth over the top, making sure the lentils are submerged. Bake for 30 minutes, or until the lentils are cooked al dente and the tomatoes are tender. Remove the dish from the oven.

Pat the fish dry with a paper towel, season with salt and pepper, and add the fillets to the dish so they fit snuggly among the lentils and veggies. Roast for 10 to 12 minutes, until the fish is cooked through and opaque. Serve immediately with a drizzle the Lemon Caper Vinaigrette over the fillets.

CRISPY CORNMEAL-DUSTED SCALLOPS WITH CHIMICHURRI

12 scallops

Sea salt

⅓ cup fine cornmeal

Freshly ground black pepper

2 tablespoons ghee or sunflower oil (or other high-heat oil)

Chimichurri + Yogurt (page 32) for serving

Where I live, scallops are plentiful, sustainable, and actually help our local ecosystem. Not to mention that they are supremely fresh and delicious. We eat a decent amount of scallops during their peak season. Another bonus is they are so quick to throw together for dinner—less than five minutes in a pan and they're done! The cornmeal crust gives them a nice outer layer of crunch, and chimichurri brings with it that green, herby goodness that makes everything taste so good. Serve these with quinoa or rice and some veggies for a complete meal.

Pat the scallops dry, and season them with salt to allow some of the moisture to be drawn out. Set them aside for 10 minutes, then pat them dry again with a paper towel. Put the cornmeal and some black pepper in a shallow bowl, and dredge the scallops in it, coating them evenly on both sides.

Heat the ghee in a cast iron pan over medium-high heat. When the pan is hot, add the scallops. You want the scallops to sizzle when they hit the pan. Cook for 1 to 2 minutes on the first side, but do not disturb or flip until they are golden brown. Then flip and cook for another 1 to 2 minutes. Transfer to a plate and serve warm with the chimichurri.

WHOLE ROASTED FISH WITH TARRAGON SALSA VERDE

½ cup extra-virgin olive oil

Zest and juice from 1 lime

2 cloves garlic, minced

1 teaspoon ground coriander

Pinch of red pepper flakes

Two 2-pound whole fish (such as snapper or branzino), cleaned and scaled

Sea salt

Freshly ground black pepper

2 handfuls of basil

2 lemons, thinly sliced

Tarragon Salsa Verde (page 34) for serving

We often make whole roasted fish at home. Sometimes we share one fish when it's the two of us, or I make a couple if I am serving friends and family. It is also one of those meals I throw together when we have last-minute guests because it is surprisingly easy to prepare and makes for a dramatic presentation. Even though it's optional, I would strongly suggest serving this with the salsa verde, because those herby, anchovy, garlic flavors only enhance a beautiful piece of fish. Of course, if you want to make this even easier and simpler, serve the fish with just some charred, roasted lemons on the side for liberal squeezing.

———————

Preheat the oven to 400°F.

Put the olive oil, lime zest and juice, garlic, coriander, and red pepper flakes in a small bowl and whisk to combine. Place the fish in a large roasting pan and season liberally with salt and pepper. Spoon the mixture all over the fish, inside the cavity as well as over the top. Stuff the basil and lemon slices around and inside the fish. Roast in the oven for 25 to 30 minutes, until cooked through. To test, remove the fish from the oven and see if it is opaque and flaking apart on the inside. When the fish is done, transfer to serving plates, and serve with the salsa verde on the side.

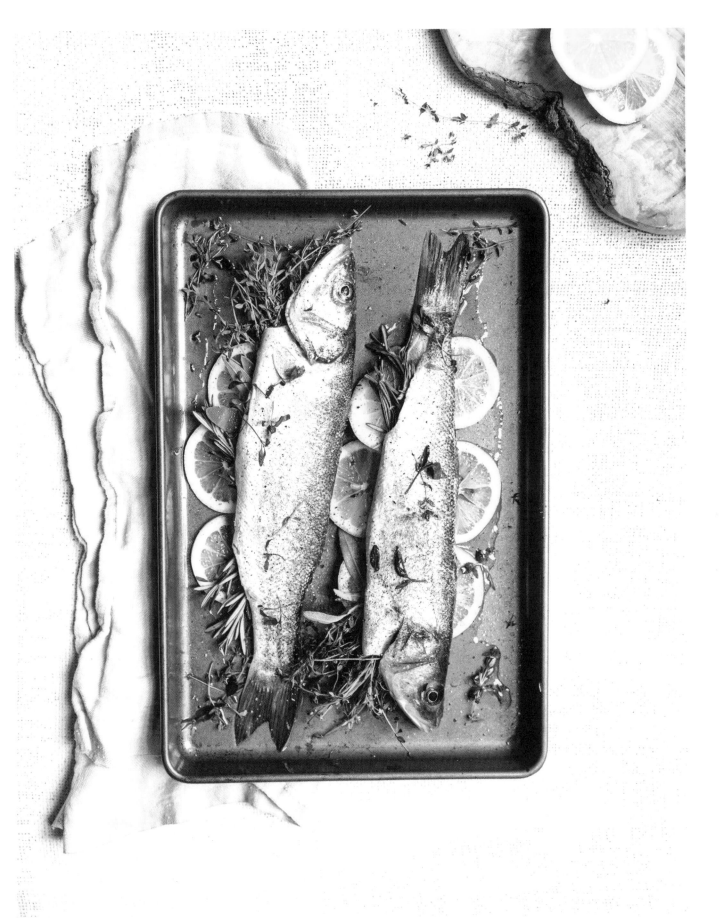

SLOW-COOKED SALMON NIÇOISE PLATTER

2 lemons, thinly sliced

Six 6-ounce pieces salmon (preferably wild-caught)

Drizzle of extra virgin olive oil

Sea salt

Freshly ground black pepper

1 pound green beans or haricots verts, trimmed

½ pound small potatoes (such as fingerling or baby russet)

6 hard-boiled eggs (optional)

Arugula or crisp salad greens for serving

Everyday Shallot + Mustard Vinaigrette (page 39)

This is the perfect dish to serve at a springtime or summer lunch or brunch. I love the idea of serving all the parts of the salmon Niçoise and allowing guests to make up their own plate. I sometimes even prepare this for my husband and myself when we have one or more of the elements, such as salmon, potatoes, or green beans, left over from the night before, making it even easier to throw together. Slow roasting the salmon in the oven is the most foolproof way to cook this fish. The slow roasting ensures that you don't overcook the salmon, so it comes out flaky, tender, and perfectly cooked every time. I encourage you to try this method, with or without the Niçoise ingredients.

———————

Preheat the oven to 300°F. Line a baking sheet with parchment and scatter the sliced lemon onto it. Place the salmon on top, skin side down, drizzle with olive oil, and season with salt and pepper. Roast for about 15 minutes, until the fish is opaque and easily flakes apart with a fork. Depending on your oven you might need a little more than 15 minutes, so keep checking back every couple of minutes until it's cooked to your liking. I prefer salmon medium-rare because I think the flavor is best, but feel free to cook longer if you want it more well done.

Bring a large pot of water to a boil. Have a large bowl with ice water nearby. Put the green beans in the boiling water and blanch for about 2 minutes. Strain, and transfer to the ice water bath until cooled. Remove, and drizzle with olive oil and season with salt and pepper.

In the same pot, add the potatoes, cover with cold water, and bring to a boil. Cook the potatoes for 10 to 15 minutes, until tender.

To serve, arrange the salmon, green beans, potatoes, hard-boiled eggs (if using), and arugula or greens onto a large serving platter with the vinaigrette on the side.

ALMOND-CRUSTED FISH TACOS WITH QUICK PICKLED CHILIES + AVOCADO MASH

Is there anything better than a taco? Just hearing the word makes me happy and brings back so many memories—from my mom's taco Tuesdays to our wedding in Mexico. The best is a fish taco with a little bit of crispness on the outside of the fish. It's also the ideal thing to make when friends come over and want to help out in the kitchen. Tacos are great to feed a crowd because they are easy to make, and people can build their own to their tastes, which means you can easily offer vegetarian options too.

Avocado Mash

2 ripe avocados

Juice of 1 lime

1 tablespoon extra virgin olive oil

3 scallions, white and light green parts only, minced

Handful of cilantro, chopped

Pinch of sea salt

Freshly ground black pepper

Fish

1 egg, lightly beaten

½ cup almonds, finely chopped

½ cup cornmeal

1 teaspoon chili powder

½ teaspoon garlic powder

½ teaspoon sea salt

Freshly ground black pepper

2 pounds white fish (such as cod or halibut)

Drizzle of olive oil

To Serve

Several soft flour or corn taco tortillas

Quick pickled red chilies (page 27)

Avocado Mash

Put the avocado, lime juice, olive oil, scallions, cilantro, salt, and pepper to taste in a medium bowl and mash the avocado until smooth and all of the ingredients are combined. Place in the fridge until you're ready to serve.

Fish

Preheat the oven to 400°F. Put the egg in a shallow bowl. Mix together the almond, cornmeal, chili powder, garlic powder, salt, and pepper to taste in another shallow bowl. Line a baking sheet with parchment. Cut the fish into 4-inch-long and 2-inch-wide pieces. Dip the fish pieces, one at a time, into the egg and then into the almond mixture, making sure each piece is evenly coated. Place them on the baking sheet and drizzle with olive oil. When all of the fish pieces have been coated, bake in the oven for 15 minutes. Transfer to a serving plate.

To assemble, place a piece or two of fish onto a tortilla, and top with a couple of pickled chilies and some avocado mash. Repeat with the remaining ingredients.

QUICK ONE-PAN MEALS = FISH + VEGGIES

All of these easy preparations use one pan to create a full and delicious meal. This is a great way to feed yourself or a crowd when you don't have a lot of time to spend making dinner, and you don't want to do a lot of dishes.

For each of these recipes, preheat the oven to 350°F. Then, simply dice the veggies, place them on a large baking tray, and toss them with a drizzle of olive oil, sea salt, and freshly ground black pepper. Roast the vegetables for 30 to 40 minutes, or until they are soft. Then, follow the specific instructions for the different fish below.

Cod

Serves 4

1 large eggplant, diced

1 pint grape tomatoes, halved

3 cloves garlic, minced

1 lemon, thinly sliced

2 pounds (4 pieces) cod
(or other firm white fish)

About 10 basil leaves,
roughly chopped

Add the lemon slices and the cod to the tray with the veggies (see above) and season the fish. Return the tray to the oven for another 15 minutes, until the fish is opaque and cooked through. Finish with the chopped basil and serve.

Halibut

Serves 4

About 4 cups peeled and cubed squash (such as butternut, acorn, or Delicata; Delicata can be left unpeeled)

4 shallots, quartered

2 pounds (4 pieces) halibut

Pesto of your choice (pages 24 to 25) for serving

Add the halibut to the tray with the veggies (see page 218), season the fish, and return to the oven for another 15 minutes, until the fish is opaque and cooked through. Finish with a spoonful of pesto over the fish.

Salmon

Serves 4

1 head broccoli, cut into florets (roast the stem too by peeling the outer layer and dicing)

2 pounds (4 pieces) salmon

Spicy Ginger Sesame Mustard (page 38) for serving

Add the salmon to the tray with the veggies (see page 218), season the fish, and return to the oven for another 15 minutes, until the fish is cooked to your liking. Finish with a spoonful of the ginger mustard over the fish.

Coconut Curry Sea Bass

Serves 4

2 sweet potatoes, peeled and diced (about 2 cups)

1 red onion, sliced

2 pounds (4 pieces) sea bass

½ cup canned full-fat coconut milk

1 tablespoon curry powder

Add the sea bass to the tray with the veggies (see page 218), season the fish, and return to the oven for another 10 minutes. Whisk together the coconut and curry, and pour it over the sweet potatoes and fish in the tray. Bake for an additional 5 minutes. Remove when the fish is opaque and cooked through, and serve.

MAPLE MUSTARD MISO MARINATED BLACK COD

¼ cup mirin

¼ cup white miso

1 tablespoon Dijon mustard

1 tablespoon maple syrup

1 to 2 pounds black cod

This recipe is inspired by the flavorful, flaky, addictive miso cod that you often find at Japanese restaurants. It's a simple preparation with spectacular results. I've served this for large family gatherings as well as for small dinner parties with friends because it's so easy but so impressive. Although you do not necessarily need to marinate your fish for more than an hour, it does taste much better if marinated up to twenty-four hours before cooking. I recommend black cod (which is much different, more delicate, and more oily than regular Atlantic cod), but you can make this with almost any kind of fish. Serve it with a simple sautéed green such as bok choy or spinach.

———

Put the mirin, miso, mustard, and maple syrup in a small bowl and whisk to combine.

Place the fish in a glass baking dish, pour the marinade over it, cover, and refrigerate. Marinate the fish for a minimum of 1 hour, or up to 24 hours. The longer the better.

When you're ready to cook, make sure the oven rack is second from the top and preheat the broiler. Transfer the fish to a baking sheet and broil for 5 to 10 minutes, until golden brown on top, opaque in the center, and easily flaking apart with a fork. Broiler times vary greatly, so check on your fish early so as not to overcook, but don't be afraid if the fish looks crisp and burned on top. That is just the sugar caramelizing, which is what you want, and it is really tasty. Transfer to a serving plate or individual plates and serve.

TURMERIC GARLIC-RUBBED FISH IN PARCHMENT

2 cloves garlic

1 teaspoon turmeric

1 teaspoon cumin

½ teaspoon cinnamon

½ teaspoon kosher salt

Pinch of cayenne

¼ cup extra virgin olive oil

Four 8-ounce pieces of white fish (such as halibut, cod, sea bass)

This turmeric garlic paste gives a tasty, healthy boost to all kinds of foods. I use the same flavorful paste with carrots on page 183, and in roasted vegetable soups, where I roast the veggies in it before blending. This recipe is great for an easy weeknight meal because the paste is simple to make, and cooking fish in parchment is a foolproof way to prepare fish perfectly. If you love this paste as much as I do, make a big batch and keep it in the fridge for a week or two—it will make this dish or any other meal even easier to throw together.

Preheat the oven to 400°F.

Put the garlic, turmeric, cumin, cinnamon, salt, cayenne, and olive oil in a food processor and blend until smooth.

Place 4 pieces of parchment (large enough to wrap the fish) on a large baking sheet. Place a piece of the fish on top of the parchment and rub it with ¼ of the rub mixture. Wrap the fish in the parchment by folding up the two long sides and rolling it down toward the fish, stopping just above the fish. Then twist the sides to keep the wrap in place. Do this to each piece of fish, arranging them in a row on the baking sheet as you go, then put the sheet in the oven for 15 minutes.

To serve, either remove from the parchment or place each piece of fish in the parchment on an individual plate. Be sure to open up the parchment or else the fish will keep cooking. Serve warm.

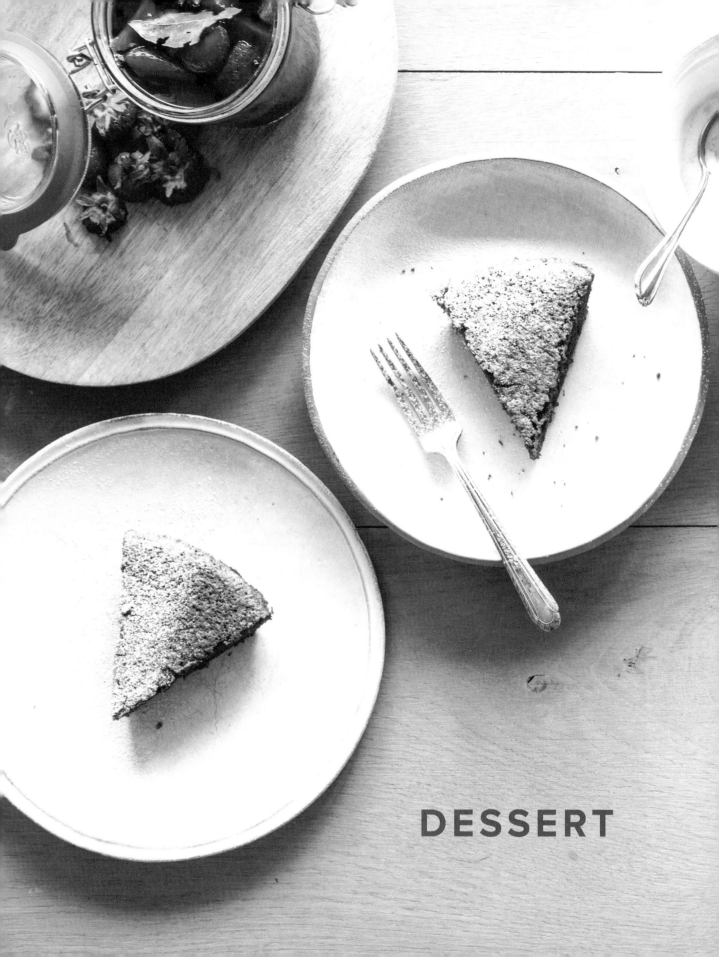

DESSERT

When it comes to dessert, I take inspiration from more traditional dishes like apple crisp, olive oil cake, and brownies, but then I like to put my own stamp on them. That means that they are made without dairy or gluten, usually without refined sugar, and with a little twist of the unexpected—like the addition of sweet white miso or tahini. I also like to sneak vegetables such as sweet potatoes and healthy fats like olive oil into my baked goods as well. I think that desserts should be filled with ingredients that not only are indulgent and delicious but also have some redeeming qualities, for good measure.

DESSERT

Rhubarb Bars   228

Pickled Strawberries   231

Lemongrass + Ginger Granita
with Salty Honey Labneh   232

Grilled Pineapple with Whipped
Coconut Cream + Honey + Basil   235

The Creamiest Dairy-Free
Ice Cream   236

    Mint   237

    Strawberry (or Any Berry!)   237

    Vanilla Bean   237

Easy Ice Cream Layer Cake   238

Raspberry + Cacao Black Rice
Pudding   241

Almond + Rosemary + Olive Oil Cake
with Figs   242

Ginger + Wine-Poached Pears
with Pine Nut Crumble   245

Caramelized Banana Pie Parfaits   246

Flourless Chocolate Blood
Orange Cake   249

Apple + Miso + Date Crisp   250

Chocolate + Tahini + Sweet Potato
Mousse   253

Strawberry Hazelnut Fudge Pops   254

RHUBARB BARS

Special Equipment:
9 x 9-inch baking pan

Crust

1 cup oat flour

1 cup brown rice flour

½ cup maple syrup

½ cup extra virgin olive oil

¼ teaspoon sea salt

Almond Rhubarb Filling

2 cups almond slivers

2 tablespoons oat flour

⅔ cup coconut palm sugar

½ cup extra virgin olive oil

½ pound (6 large stalks) rhubarb, cut in half lengthwise

I know I have a lot of favorites when it comes to food, but rhubarb is one of my true loves. Rhubarb can be used in so many ways, but these bars are just the best. Since rhubarb is super-seasonal, I usually stock up when I can and store it in a bag in the freezer (it keeps well frozen). If you do not have rhubarb or it's not in season, you can make this recipe with any sliced fruit or berries. Peaches, blueberries, or apples would all make wonderful substitutes.

————————

Preheat the oven to 350°F. Line the baking pan with two pieces of parchment paper, going in different directions, enough to come up and over each side (this will make them easy to remove).

Crust
In a large mixing bowl, add the oat flour, brown rice flour, maple syrup, olive oil, and salt and stir to combine. Transfer the mixture to the parchment-lined pan and press evenly on all sides. Bake for 10 minutes, remove, and allow to cool slightly while you prepare the filling.

Almond Rhubarb Filling
Put the almonds on a baking sheet and toast in the oven for 5 to 10 minutes, until golden brown. Transfer the almonds to a food processor and add the oat flour, sugar, and olive oil and pulse several times until you have a coarse but consistent mixture. Spread the mixture evenly on top of the crust. Arrange the rhubarb on top, any way you like.

Return the pan to the oven and bake for another 30 to 35 minutes, until the rhubarb is soft and cooked through. Let the pan cool for at least 15 minutes before attempting to remove the bars and cutting into them. Once ready, lift the parchment out of the pan and transfer to a flat surface to cut the bars into squares. The bars will keep for several days on the countertop in an airtight container.

PICKLED STRAWBERRIES

Special Equipment:
Large glass mason jar for storing

1 cup red wine vinegar

1 cup water

4 tablespoons white granulated sugar

1 teaspoon sea salt

1 teaspoon whole black peppercorns

1 cinnamon stick

1 vanilla bean, seeds scraped

1 bay leaf

4 cloves

2 pieces lemon zest (about 1 inch long)

2 cups ripe strawberries, hulled and halved

Other fruits that would be fun to pickle:

- Peaches + Fennel seed

- Plums + Coriander seed

- Raspberries + Mint

- Cherries + Chili flakes

- Blueberries + Jalapeño

I took a canning and preserving class at Stone Barns Center, in New York's Hudson Valley, hoping that I could then put my canning set to use. I learned a few things—pickling is easier than canning, and you can actually pickle sweet, lovely fruits like strawberries. Who knew? Pickled strawberries are sweet and sour and go so well over so many things, but the best part is you can pickle them when they are in season and then get to enjoy them for months after. I like to make a big jar of these and store them in the fridge, saving them to serve over ice cream, with cake, on pancakes or crepes, and in cocktails.

———————

Place the vinegar, water, sugar, salt, peppercorns, cinnamon stick, vanilla, bay leaf, cloves, and lemon zest in a large, heavy-bottomed pot and simmer over medium-high heat for 10 minutes. Put the hulled strawberries in the mason jar, or any jar with an airtight lid. Pour the hot brine over the strawberries, filling the jar to ¼ inch below the rim. Make sure you get all of the spices into the jar as well. Set aside, uncovered, and allow it to cool completely to room temperature. Cover with a tight-fitting lid and keep in the fridge when not in use. These will last for a couple of months in the fridge.

LEMONGRASS + GINGER GRANITA WITH
SALTY HONEY LABNEH

Special Equipment:
Cheesecloth

1 cup 2% fat plain Greek sheep,
goat, or coconut milk yogurt

½ teaspoon Maldon sea salt
or kosher salt

1 tablespoon honey

8 stalks lemongrass,
cut into 3-inch pieces

2-inch piece ginger,
peeled and sliced

1 cup white granulated sugar

Juice of ½ lemon or 1 lime
(about 1 tablespoon)

4½ cups water

Granola for serving (optional)

Dried fruit (such as blueberries or
pomegranates) for serving (optional)

Granita is a sweet, frozen, fruit-flavored dessert from Sicily, also known as Italian ice where I grew up. You make it by simply combining sugar, water, and a fruit or herb of your choice. Labneh is a Middle Eastern soft yogurt cheese. It has the same tangy taste as yogurt but with a thicker consistency. If you like you can make it dairy-free by choosing a nondairy yogurt such as coconut or almond milk. This dessert is incredibly easy to make, but it takes about a day of freezing and straining, so be sure to plan ahead.

————————

One to two days before serving, begin making the labneh. Place a colander over a bowl, and drape a large piece of cheesecloth over the colander. Put the yogurt on top of the cheesecloth, and gather the edges to cover the yogurt. Put in the fridge for 24 to 48 hours. Remove, and squeeze the cheesecloth tightly to strain any excess liquid from the yogurt. Stir in the salt and honey, and place in fridge, covered, until you're ready to serve.

The morning (or a minimum of 5 hours) before you would like to serve the dessert, make the granita. Put the lemongrass, ginger, sugar, lemon juice, and water into a medium saucepan and bring to a boil. Once it comes to a boil, stir until the sugar has dissolved, then remove it from the heat and allow it to sit and steep while it comes to room temperature. Once cooled completely, strain it into a small or medium glass baking dish or a loaf pan. Place in the freezer for 3 hours, then remove and scrape the mixture with a fork to create chunks of ice. Do this every couple of hours until you're ready to serve.

To serve, place a spoonful of the labneh at the bottom of each bowl, and top with a spoonful of the granita. Sprinkle with granola and dried fruit, if using, or any additional topping that you like. Serve chilled.

GRILLED PINEAPPLE WITH WHIPPED
COCONUT CREAM + HONEY + BASIL

One 13½-ounce can full-fat coconut milk, placed upside down in the fridge for a minimum of 4 hours or overnight

2 tablespoons powdered sugar

½ teaspoon vanilla extract

10 basil leaves, roughly chopped

1 medium pineapple, cut into 2-inch-thick triangles

3 tablespoons honey + more for drizzling

Puffed rice for serving (optional; page 74)

Toasted nuts or coconut for serving (optional)

When the weather is warm, we tend to do more entertaining. We always serve dessert, but when it's hot out, who wants a heavy, indulgent dessert after a big meal? Grilled pineapple is the solution. It is so simple to make, with little prep involved, and the results are so delicious. Just be sure to put the can of coconut milk in the fridge upside down several hours before whipping. I keep an upside-down can of coconut milk in the fridge as a pantry staple, so I am always prepared to whip up some coconut cream.

Open the chilled can of coconut milk. Skim off the solid coconut cream on top and put it in a large mixing bowl or bowl of a stand mixer. Reserve the liquid that remains in the bottom of the can for another use (such as a smoothie). Add the sugar and vanilla to the bowl and whip for about 1 minute, until the mixture is frothy and creamy. Stir in the basil, and immediately place in the fridge until ready to serve.

Preheat the grill to medium-high heat. Put the pineapple in a large bowl, drizzle with the honey, and toss to coat. Cook the pineapple for 3 to 5 minutes on each side, until charred and caramelized.

Place the pineapple on individual plates or a serving platter. If serving in a platter, offer the coconut cream on the side (chilled if it's really hot out), so it won't melt. If serving individually, then place a dollop of the cream next to the skewer, drizzle some extra honey over the top, and finish with puffed rice, toasted nuts or coconut, if using, or any other toppings you like.

THE CREAMIEST DAIRY-FREE
ICE CREAM

Special Equipment:
Ice cream maker

4 egg yolks

½ cup white granulated
or coconut palm sugar

½ teaspoon sea salt

Two 13½-ounce cans full
fat coconut milk

Here are a few great combinations to try out, but feel free to experiment on your own with your favorite flavors.

- Mint + Chocolate chip
- Rhubarb + Pistachio
- Strawberry + Basil
- Vanilla bean + Bourbon
- Peach + Mint

It took me a long time to get over the intimidation factor of making ice cream. Yes, you need a bit of patience, but it is actually a very easy process. To do it properly, you need an ice cream maker or the ice cream bowl attachment for your stand mixer, but if you love homemade ice cream, as I do, it is well worth the investment. The recipe involves only a few steps, but keep in mind you'll need several hours of chill time. Since I steer clear of cream, I have experimented only with dairy-free ice cream bases, and I am blown away by the results. This wonderful version uses a more traditional ice cream–making technique involving egg yolks for the custard, and in lieu of the cream, I use coconut milk. The result is a creamy, luscious ice cream that is a great starting point for exploring all kinds of flavor additions.

Put the egg yolks, sugar, and salt in a large saucepan (not over heat yet), and whisk until combined. Pour the coconut milk over the egg mixture and whisk until combined. Place the pan over medium heat, and cook while whisking frequently, about 10 to 15 minutes, until a custard has formed (basically until the mixture thickens enough to coat the back of a spoon). Transfer the mixture to a glass mixing bowl, cool to room temperature, cover, and place in the fridge for a minimum of 4 hours, or ideally overnight.

Using an ice cream maker, churn the ice cream according to the ice cream maker's instructions or continuously for about 20 to 25 minutes. When the ice cream is done churning, transfer to a container to store in the freezer (preferably with a lid) or enjoy immediately from the ice cream maker (this is when the ice cream will be best!).

Mint

First, steep 1 cup of fresh mint leaves in the coconut milk for 2 hours before straining and adding the coconut milk to the egg yolk mixture. Then follow the rest of the main recipe instructions.

Strawberry (or Any Berry!)

First, cook down 4 cups of hulled strawberries with 2 teaspoons vanilla extract in the coconut milk over medium heat, and allow it to cool to room temperature before adding it to the egg yolk mixture. Then follow the rest of the main recipe instructions.

Vanilla Bean

First, scrape the seeds from 2 vanilla beans into the coconut milk and steep, along with the pods, in the coconut milk for about 2 hours. Remove the vanilla pod and add the flavored coconut milk to the egg yolk mixture. Then follow the rest of the main recipe instructions.

EASY ICE CREAM LAYER CAKE

Special Equipment:
8 x 4-inch loaf pan

1 cup gluten-free flour

¼ cup coconut flour

2 teaspoons baking powder

½ teaspoon sea salt

⅓ cup sunflower oil

¾ cup maple syrup

¾ cup unsweetened almond or cashew milk (page 70)

3 tablespoons vanilla extract

2 eggs, lightly beaten

1 quart ice cream of your choice (I like dairy-free vanilla ice cream)

Note: Coconut flour is not easily substituted since it absorbs liquid much more than any other flour, so be careful if you decide to experiment and sub it out—the ratios will likely be very different.

My mom's homemade ice cream cake was a staple at my birthday parties for many years. I wanted to come up with a super-easy way to make this nostalgic dessert, and the version here is something you can easily throw together in a flash for a birthday party, dinner party, or just to satisfy a craving. The cake has a slight coconut flavor thanks to the coconut flour, so be sure to consider this when choosing your ice cream flavor.

Preheat the oven to 350°F. Grease the loaf pan.

In a medium bowl, whisk together the gluten-free flour, coconut flour, baking powder, and salt. In another bowl, whisk together the oil, maple syrup, milk, vanilla, and eggs. Pour the wet mixture in with the dry mixture, and whisk until combined. Pour into the loaf pan, and bake for 25 to 30 minutes. Remove and allow to cool for at least 30 minutes before handling.

Take the ice cream out of the freezer. When the cake has cooled, flip it onto a plate and allow it to cool for another 10 minutes while the ice cream softens. Carefully cut the cake in half, horizontally. Line the inside of the (now empty) loaf pan with plastic wrap, leaving extra to hang over the edges—this is how you will remove the cake from the pan once it's frozen. Place the bottom slice of cake back into the pan. Scoop the entire quart of ice cream and place it onto the bottom piece of cake. Smooth it out with a spatula, making an even layer. Add the top piece of cake, and place the pan in the fridge for 4 hours or overnight. About 10 minutes before serving, remove the pan from the freezer, and then gently lift the cake out and transfer to a serving plate. Cut individual slices to serve.

This is best served within a day or so of making, since the cake gets too hard if it hangs out in the freezer for a long time.

RASPBERRY + CACAO BLACK RICE PUDDING

Special Equipment:
8 x 8-inch baking dish

3 cups frozen raspberries

Drizzle of maple syrup

2 teaspoons vanilla extract

1 cup black rice, rinsed well

Pinch of sea salt

3 cups water

One 13½-ounce can full fat coconut milk

⅓ cup coconut palm sugar

1 tablespoon cacao powder

My mom used to make an amazing rice pudding for me when I was a kid. She continued to prepare it for me as an adult, when I was sick or just needed a little extra love—she even started making it with almond milk when I cut out dairy from my diet. I always thought of rice pudding as a classic dish until my mom started switching it up, and it got me thinking of all the different ways rice pudding could be made: various kinds of rice, the addition of a fruit, all types of milk. This recipe is a fun twist on my mom's traditional rice pudding, using black rice instead of white and coconut milk instead of dairy. The cacao and raspberries are extras and can be left out if you prefer, but I think the combination of chocolate and raspberry with this black rice pudding takes it to another level.

———————

Preheat the oven to 400°F. Put the raspberries, maple syrup, and 1 teaspoon of the vanilla in the baking dish. Bake for 20 to 25 minutes, until the raspberries are soft and bubbly. Remove and allow to cool while you cook the rice.

Put the rice, salt, and water into a medium saucepan. Bring to a boil, cover, reduce to a simmer, and cook for 40 minutes or until the rice is cooked but there is still liquid in the pot. Uncover, and add the coconut milk, sugar, cacao powder, and the remaining teaspoon of vanilla and cook, stirring occasionally, until the mixture is thick and creamy, about 30 minutes. Pour the coconut rice mixture over the raspberries, and allow to cool before serving, or you can transfer to the fridge and allow it to cool completely before serving. The pudding will keep in the fridge, covered, for several days.

ALMOND + ROSEMARY + OLIVE OIL CAKE WITH FIGS

Special Equipment:
9-inch round cake pan

¼ cup good-quality extra virgin olive oil + more for greasing the pan

4 large eggs

½ cup white granulated sugar

1½ cups almond flour

1 teaspoon baking powder

½ teaspoon baking soda

½ teaspoon sea salt

1 tablespoon dried, ground rosemary

Zest from 1 lemon

¼ cup freshly squeezed lemon juice

1 dozen fresh figs, thinly sliced (optional)

Ice cream for serving (optional)

I have a love affair with olive oil cake, which I refer to as my "adult" cake. And by adult cake, I mean it leans more toward the savory and salty side than the sweet. The flavor of the olive oil really shines here, which is why you want to choose an oil that you truly enjoy. I tend to like strong-tasting olive oils with a fruity finish, but feel free to pick whichever kind you prefer. You might want to serve this cake at a fancy tea with friends, but it's so simple to make that I sometimes just bake it for myself to enjoy as a snack all week long. If you don't have figs on hand or they are out of season, leave them out or play around with other fruits. Dates, thinly sliced pears, or stone fruits like plums are all great options.

———————

Preheat the oven to 350°F. Grease the cake pan with olive oil, cut out a piece of parchment paper and put it in the bottom of the pan, and set aside.

Put the olive oil, eggs, and sugar in the bowl of a stand mixer with a whisk attachment and whisk on high for a couple of minutes, until a thick cream has formed (it should coat the back of the spoon). Meanwhile, put the almond flour, baking soda, salt, and rosemary in a large bowl and whisk to combine. Pour the olive oil mixture into the dry ingredients and stir to incorporate. Add the lemon zest and juice and stir until incorporated.

Pour the mixture into the cake pan, and place the sliced figs on top. Bake for about 35 to 40 minutes, until a cake tester comes out clean. Allow it to rest for 10 minutes, then remove the cake from the pan and allow it to cool on a rack for another 10 to 15 minutes before slicing. Serve this slightly warm with a scoop of ice cream, if using. This cake will keep for several days covered on the countertop.

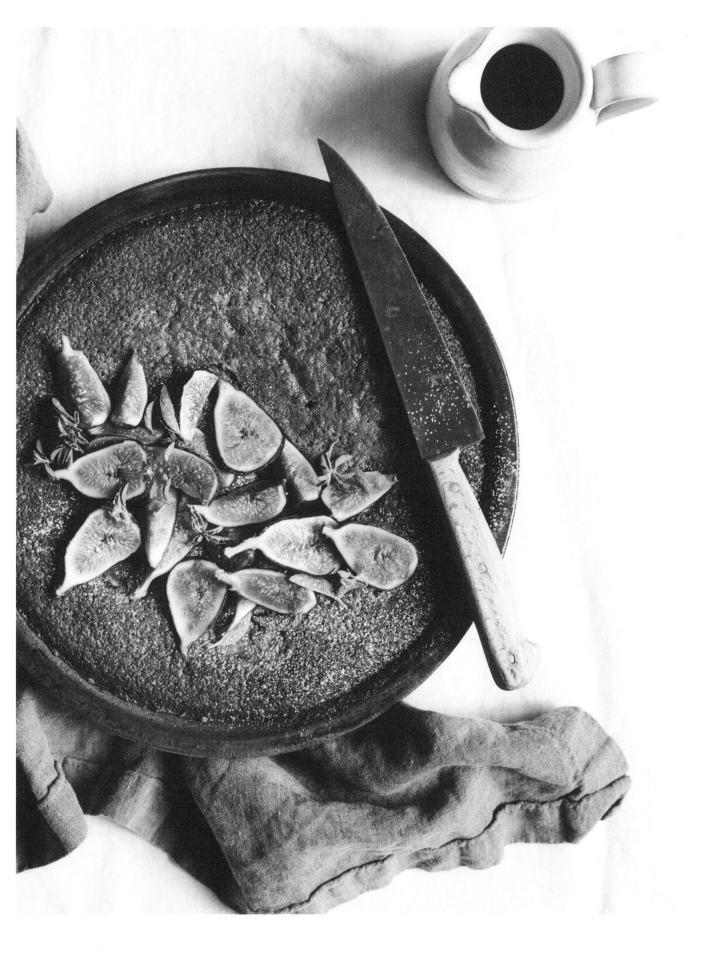

GINGER + WINE-POACHED PEARS WITH PINE NUT CRUMBLE

½ cup rolled oats

⅓ cup oat flour

½ teaspoon sea salt

¼ teaspoon cinnamon

¼ cup extra-virgin olive oil

⅓ cup pine nuts, roughly chopped

One 12-ounce bottle sweet white dessert wine

2-inch piece of ginger, peeled and sliced

¼ cup maple syrup

3 or 4 pears, peeled, halved, and cored

Ice cream or coconut whipped cream for serving

Whenever I have family or friends over for dinner, dessert will always be served. It doesn't have to be anything complicated—sometimes it is as simple as grilled fruit with coconut cream. When weather turns cooler and the grill is off for the season, this is a simple, low-fuss dessert. You can use any kind white wine you have on hand if you don't have dessert wine, and have fun experimenting with other fruits such as peaches, plums, or apricots.

———————

Preheat the oven to 325°F.

Mix together the rolled oats, oat flour, salt, cinnamon, and olive oil in a medium bowl. Spread the mixture onto a small baking sheet. Bake for 10 minutes, remove, add the pine nuts, and return to the oven for another 5 minutes, until everything is golden and crisp. Set aside until you're ready to serve.

Put the wine, ginger, and maple syrup into a medium, deep pan. Bring to a gentle simmer over medium-low heat and whisk to dissolve the syrup. Add the pears, cut side up, and simmer for 10 minutes. Flip the pears carefully using tongs and cook for another 10 minutes. Transfer the pears to small, shallow serving bowls, and top with a sprinkle of the crumble, a scoop of ice cream, and a drizzle of the cooking juices.

CARAMELIZED BANANA PIE PARFAITS

½ cup rolled oats

½ cup cashews

Pinch of sea salt

1 tablespoon maple syrup

2 tablespoons coconut oil

4 ripe bananas, cut
into 1-inch pieces

2 tablespoons ghee or
grapeseed oil (or other neutral
high-heat oil)

Ice cream, cashew yogurt,
or coconut whip for serving

Caramelized banana is a beloved indulgence of mine. Heating and coaxing the sugars out of the banana for a caramel crispy crust completely transforms this fruit into something so decadent and delicious—and magically, without the addition of sugar. When layers of crumbly bits that taste like pie crust are added between layers of the sweet banana, this treat tastes like it should be so bad but it is actually good for you. Be creative or use what you have, for even more layers of flavor. You could top this off with a scoop of vanilla ice cream or a spoonful of cashew or coconut yogurt.

———————

Preheat the oven to 350°F.

Put the oats, cashews, and salt into a food processor and pulse several times, until a fine meal has formed. Then add the maple syrup and coconut oil and pulse until you have a dough-like consistency. Spread the mixture out on a parchment-lined baking sheet, and bake for 15 to 20 minutes, until golden brown. Set aside while you prepare the parfaits. Alternatively, you can make this a couple of days in advance and store in an airtight container in the fridge.

When you're ready to assemble the parfaits (which I recommend you do shortly before serving), caramelize the bananas. Heat the ghee or oil in a medium frying pan and add the bananas. Cook, undisturbed, for 3 to 5 minutes on one side, until they are browned and caramelized. Flip, and cook for another 3 to 5 minutes on the other side, then remove from the heat.

Assemble the parfaits. Using a few small to medium glasses, jars, or bowls, begin to layer the ingredients starting with a spoonful of the pie crust, then a spoonful of banana, then another layer of the pie crust, and another layer of banana, and top it off with a scoop of ice cream, cashew yogurt, or coconut whip. Serve shortly after assembling.

FLOURLESS CHOCOLATE BLOOD ORANGE CAKE

Special Equipment:
9-inch round cake pan

⅔ cup extra virgin olive oil + more for greasing the pan

⅓ cup cocoa powder + more for dusting (optional)

1 tablespoon vanilla extract

½ cup freshly squeezed blood orange or regular orange juice

1 cup coconut palm sugar

3 large eggs

1½ cups almond flour

½ teaspoon baking soda

¼ teaspoon sea salt

Powdered sugar for dusting (optional)

Who doesn't love a flourless chocolate cake? The idea of a moist, decadent, chocolaty cake without the guilt of the flour weighing it down sounds perfect to me . . . except for the dairy. Happily, it turns out that olive oil makes for a really delicious substitute for the butter typically used in a more traditional flourless chocolate cake, and the orange juice gives it that extra fresh little zing.

———

Preheat the oven to 350°F. Grease the cake pan with olive oil, and line the bottom with parchment paper.

Put the cocoa powder and vanilla in a small mixing bowl, pour the orange juice over it, and whisk to combine. Set aside.

Put the sugar, eggs, and olive oil in the bowl of a stand mixer with the whisk attachment, and whisk on high until a thick cream has formed (it should be thick enough to coat the back of a spoon). Turn the speed down to low, and add in the cocoa liquid. Slowly add in the almond flour, then the baking soda and salt. Whisk for another minute, until fully combined.

Pour the batter into the cake pan and bake for 35 to 40 minutes, until a cake tester comes out clean when poked in the center. Allow it to cool for 10 to 15 minutes on a wire rack, then remove the cake from the pan and allow it to cool further on the rack. Serve slightly warm with a dusting of cocoa powder and/or powdered sugar, if using.

APPLE + MISO + DATE CRISP

Special Equipment:
9 x 9-inch baking dish

6 apples, peeled, cored, and thinly sliced

7 dates, pitted and diced

¼ cup coconut palm sugar

2 tablespoons almond flour

Juice of ½ lemon
(about 1 tablespoon)

½ teaspoon cinnamon

½ cup coconut oil

½ cup white granulated or coconut palm sugar

1 cup oat flour

½ cup almond flour

¼ cup sweet white miso

Vanilla ice cream for serving

Miso might seem like an odd ingredient for a crisp, but the first time I had miso in a dessert (a chocolate chip cookie) I was completely blown away. It was so rich and so addictive, I discovered that when miso is hidden in baked goods, it somehow adds a buttery taste without the addition of butter. After this revelation, I was inspired to come up with a recipe for an apple and date crisp with sweet miso, because I knew that the apples would embrace the miso, and the miso would add that rich, buttery flavor while remaining dairy-free. Crisps are an easy way to feed a crowd and are a great vehicle for using the best seasonal fruit. Also, the leftovers are always just as good and sometimes even better. You can find apples year-round, but feel free to make this with pears or any stone fruit.

Preheat the oven to 350°F.

Put the apples, dates, coconut palm sugar, almond flour, lemon juice, and cinnamon in the baking dish and toss to combine. Set aside while you make the topping.

In a food processor, combine the coconut oil, sugar, oat flour, almond flour, and miso and pulse several times until you have a crumbly, uniform mixture. Spread the mixture evenly over the apples and bake for 45 to 50 minutes. Allow to cool for about 10 minutes before serving. Serve warm with a scoop of vanilla ice cream.

CHOCOLATE + TAHINI + SWEET POTATO MOUSSE

2 medium sweet potatoes

½ cup cocoa powder

½ cup maple syrup

2 tablespoons tahini + more for drizzling on top

¼ teaspoon sea salt

Sneaking sweet potato into a dessert not only gets you to eat more vegetables, it is also the secret to making this mousse super-silky smooth. The nuttiness of tahini pairs so well with the richness of the chocolate, and with only a few ingredients, this dessert is as impressive and tasty as it is easy to make. Another bonus is that it only takes minutes in the food processor once your sweet potato has been roasted.

———————

Preheat the oven to 400°F. Using a fork, poke a bunch of holes into the sweet potatoes, place them on a baking sheet, and roast in the oven for 30 to 40 minutes, until the flesh is cooked through and soft. When the sweet potato is cool enough to handle, cut in half and scoop the flesh out from the skin and into a food processor. Add the cocoa powder, maple syrup, tahini, and salt. Run the food processor until the mixture is smooth. Spoon the mousse into individual serving bowls, and top with a drizzle of tahini. Store in the fridge if not enjoying right away. This will keep for several days in an airtight container in the fridge.

STRAWBERRY HAZELNUT FUDGE POPS

Special Equipment:
Ice pop molds (2 molds that hold 6 pops)

1 cup cocoa powder

1 cup coconut palm sugar

2 tablespoons tapioca starch

2 teaspoons vanilla extract

¼ teaspoon sea salt

3 cups hazelnut milk or any kind of milk (page 70)

½ cup thinly sliced strawberries (fresh or frozen)

Homemade is always better, especially in the case of ice pops—you can get super-creative with the flavors and make a big batch to keep around for snacking. Strawberries, hazelnuts, and chocolate are a dreamy combination of flavors, but if you don't feel like making a fresh batch of hazelnut milk for these, coconut, almond, or any kind of milk would be a fine substitute.

———————

Put the cocoa powder, sugar, starch, vanilla, and salt into a medium saucepan, and slowly pour in the milk while whisking constantly to keep the starch from clumping. Heat the mixture over medium-low heat and bring to a simmer, whisking continuously, until the mixture begins to bubble. Stir in the strawberries, then remove the pan from the heat. Transfer the mixture to a container with a pourer and pour the mixture into the ice pop mold. Follow the instructions for your individual mold for the sticks as well as for removing the ice pops once they are frozen. Freeze the pops for a minimum of 5 hours, or ideally overnight.

Acknowledgments

Thank you.

There are no words that can express the gratitude I have for my family, friends, and colleagues who have encouraged me, helped me out, lifted me up, and calmed me down through the creation of this book. A little piece of this book belongs to each one of you.

To my Michael. You are my rock and my biggest cheerleader. I wouldn't be doing what I love if it weren't for your constant energetic encouragement, and I don't know how I would survive without your advice, your open ears, and your big heart. You are my chief recipe tester, my late-night grocery runner, my dishwasher, my sous-chef, and the best chimichurri maker I know. This book would not have been possible without you. I love you.

To Alex and Henry. You are my favorite food critics and recipe tasters. Thanks for always being willing to try even my most "experimental vegan meals" and for testing some of my recipes (shakshuka!).

To Matt. Even though we have never had the same taste in food, we can always agree on one thing: Bolognese for life.

To Bill and Mable. Thank you for being the best role models for as long as I can remember. Our shared love for food, art, and design has always inspired me and has helped shape me into the person I am today.

To Aunt Carole. You are the foundation of the family and have always been one of my biggest fans . . . even if you don't always love the kind of food that I make. I love you lots.

To Cristina, Ramiro, Sandra, and Daniella. Thanks for treating me like family from the very beginning, and for always being so supportive of my career and journey in food. For all of the thoughtful cookbooks, recipe clippings, kitchen gadgets, and garden tips you've shared with me, and for letting me cook so many of our family meals—I am so lucky to be a part of your loving family.

To my editor, Juree, and everyone at Roost. I couldn't have asked for a better team to help me bring this book to life—it truly has been a dream come true. Juree, your thoughtful critiques have helped fine-tune and shape this book into something I couldn't be more proud of. It's really special when you get to work with someone who shares the same vision as you do. So, from the bottom of my heart, thank you.

To Chloe and Sappho. This book did not feel real until the three of us spent two weeks together, cooking and photographing every single recipe. Your talents made this book come alive and gave the pages life, and your friendship through the process made this whole experience that much more fun.

To my agent, Brandi. Thank you for believing in me, guiding me, and pushing me to develop the concept for this book from the very beginning, when it was just a title and a couple of tag lines.

To my wonderful, supportive, and inspiring group of friends. You know who you are. For always encouraging me, sharing and making my recipes, and loving my food, even back when it wasn't so tasty (hello, garlic clove mashed potatoes).

To Laura and Sarah. Thank you for being the best friends and sounding boards a girl could ask for. Laura, for being the amazing creative being that you are, and for always having an incredible assortment of linens and gorgeous props that I can steal from you. And Sarah, the best writer I know, for letting me run sentences and ideas by you that just didn't make any sense. I love you both so much.

To Hetty. Your friendship has meant so much to me, and even more so during the process of creating this book. Your advice has made me feel more grounded, and all the lunches and laughs always make everything feel lighter. I am so happy you moved to Brooklyn. There are so many more food adventures in our future.

To Joann and Gabriel. Even though we live so far apart, our constant chats keep me inspired and laughing almost every day. Thanks for letting me drag you to Amagansett so you could take some gorgeous photos of me for the book. I can't wait until we meet up and create together again (and eat late-night French-fry-and-hot-dog American pizza).

To Grounded. I thank you for keeping me caffeinated, with your almond milk lattes, and fed (when I couldn't cook one more thing), with your vegan banana bread and green smoothies, while I worked in the back way past the allotted time limit.

Last, I dedicate this book to my mom. She was my biggest fan and my best friend. She was the person who gave me my love for food and vegetables, and taught me everything she knew about being a great home cook. Although she's not here today to see this book come to life, I know she's somewhere watching and that she must be over the moon with joy and pride. This book, and every recipe in it, is for you, Mom. I love you.

Resources

ONLINE HEALTHY FOOD / NATURAL FOODS MARKETPLACE

Thrive Market—An online market where you can find many organic and natural foods, as well as health, beauty, and other products all in one place.
thrivemarket.com

PRODUCE / FARM STANDS AND FARMERS' MARKETS

The Union Square Greenmarket—A year around farmers' market, with a great variety of vendors, located in Union Square, NYC, that is open Mondays, Wednesdays, Fridays, and Saturdays.
www.grownyc.org/

Balsam Farms—A seasonal farm stand located in Amagansett, NY, that is my go-to for summer produce.
balsamfarms.com

Amber Waves—A woman-owned seasonal farm stand located in Amagansett, NY. They also have a pizza oven and host many farm dinners throughout the summer.
www.amberwavesfarm.org

Green Thumb Organic—Another seasonal farm stand located in Watermill, NY. This is where some of my sprouted plants for my summer garden come from.
greenthumborganicfarm.com

SPECIALTY STORES

SOS Chefs—My favorite specialty store for everyday spices and unique finds. They also carry some of my favorite olive oils and vinegars.
sos-chefs.com

Chelsea Market Basket—A store located in the Chelsea Market in NYC that carries special imported sauces, mustards, anchovies, and more.
www.chelseamarketbasket.com

FLOURS

Bob's Red Mill—The best place to go for alternative flours, including: oat flour, rolled oats, brown rice flour, gluten-free flour blend, and almond flour (meal).
www.bobsredmill.com

Arrowhead Mills—A great brand for all types of organic alternative baking flours.
www.arrowheadmills.com

JAPANESE PRODUCTS / SEAWEED + MISO

South River Miso Company—They have a variety of really tasty, and sometimes unique, miso blends, including a soy-free chickpea miso.
www.southrivermiso.com

Eden Foods—My go-to for organic seaweeds, gomasio, brown rice vinegar, and apple cider vinegar.
www.edenfoods.com

SUPERFOOD PRODUCTS

Navitas Naturals—A large variety of packaged superfoods including goji berries, maca powder, and cacao nibs. They also make great powdered smoothie enhancers.
navitasnaturals.com

Moon Juice Shop—Amazing superfood blends, powders, and snacks.
www.moonjuiceshop.com

COCONUT AND OTHER DAIRY SUBSTITUTES

Native Forest—My favorite brand for canned and creamed coconut milk products.

Notmilk—The best, most pure line of dairy-free nut milks, made only from nuts and water.
www.notmilknyc.com

Califia Farms—Another favorite nut milk brand. They produce several kinds of nut milks, including almond and coconut milk and they also make great (carrageenan-free) milk specifically for coffee.
www.califiafarms.com

GRAINS + BEANS

Bob's Red Mill—They are also my go-to for grains and beans. I often stock up on their quinoa, oats, buckwheat, and beans.
www.bobsredmill.com

Lundberg Farms—A variety of rice, from white rice to black rice, and rice products such as brown rice syrup.
www.lundberg.com

Ranchero Gordo—Beautiful, colorful heirloom beans, grown on the West Coast of the US.
www.ranchogordo.com

NUTS + SEEDS

Woodstock—A variety of packed nuts and seeds. They also have a great selection of frozen fruits and vegetables.
www.woodstock-foods.com

Seed + Mill—They make my favorite tahini. They use freshly milled sesame seeds, and they also have a couple of variations and flavors.
www.seedandmill.com

Justin's— A delicious selection of nut butters, almond butter, peanut butter, and my favorite chocolate peanut butter cups.
justins.com

Index

About the Author

Jodi Moreno is a NYC and Amagansett, NY based natural foods chef and creator of the acclaimed blog whatscookinggoodlooking.com, which has been named twice by *Saveur* magazine as best overall cooking blog, has been featured as blog of the year by PBS, and nominated as best in healthy cooking by *Better Homes and Gardens*. Her work has also been featured by *Vogue*, *Bon Appétit*, Food52, and more. Jodi is the co-owner of Neighborhood Studio, which is a communal kitchen, dining, and event space in Brooklyn, NY.

Photo by Glen Allsop.

Roost Books
An imprint of Shambhala Publications, Inc.
4720 Walnut Street
Boulder, Colorado 80301
roostbooks.com

9 8 7 6 5 4 3 2 1

First Edition
Printed in the United States of America

⊗This edition is printed on acid-free paper that meets the
American National Standards Institute Z39.48 Standard.
♻Shambhala Publications makes every effort to print
on recycled paper. For more information please visit
www.shambhala.com.

Distributed in the United States by Penguin Random House LLC
and in Canada by Random House of Canada Ltd

Designed by Nami Kurita

Library of Congress Cataloging-in-Publication Data
Names: Moreno, Jodi, author.
Title: More with less: whole food cooking made irresistibly
simple/Jodi Moreno.
Description: First edition. | Boulder: Roost, [2018] | Includes
bibliographical references and index.
Identifiers:LCCN 2017016263 | ISBN 9781611804706 (hardcover:
alk. paper)
Subjects: LCSH: Quick and easy cooking. | Natural foods. |
LCGFT: Cookbooks.
Classification: LCC TX833.5 .M674 2018 | DDC 641.3/02—dc23
LC record available at https://lccn.loc.gov/2017016263